Praise for
Our Common Ground

"At a time when too many people engaged in public life are talking past each other, Diane Hessan makes a very strong case for doing less of that and much more listening. Common ground is not a dirty word. Most of the time, it is where lasting, positive change comes from. People agree with each other far more often than the snark on various media platforms would imply. The people who talk to Diane and to each other give me hope. They are where the best selves of this nation will come from."

—Charlie Baker, governor of Massachusetts

"Diane has been that unique voice that is truly informed by real voters across the country and across the political spectrum. Her tremendous skill of getting people to share, candidly and often, how they really feel and respond to political moments enables her to analyze and write, with balanced perspective, about what is really happening in people's hearts and minds. This book is must-read insight into the mind of American voters."

—Linda Henry, CEO, the Boston Globe

"As a member of Congress who was on the House Floor the day the angry political mob attacked the US Capitol, you better believe I have a vested interest in moving our political dialogue to a better and more civil place. Diane Hessan and her book *Our Common Ground*—if read, discussed, absorbed, and acted on—offer one way to do that."

—**Cheri Bustos,** US Congresswoman from Illinois

"A simple lesson in human interaction—the importance of listening as a gateway to understanding and the foundation for bridging differences—is the cornerstone of Hessan's timely and hopeful book. *Our Common Ground* is a how-to for modern politics from an expert in human interaction, for a change, instead of conventional politics."

—**Deval Patrick,** former governor of Massachusetts

"If there's an expert on the undecided voter, it's Diane Hessan, who embedded herself with this 'kingmaker' group. We discover that former FBI Director James B. Comey didn't cause Secretary Hillary Clinton's loss. Clinton caused it when she fatefully said, 'a basket of deplorables.' Hessan uncovers how politicians misinform voters about each other, how the media unwittingly helps them, and how we can take back our national unity. This is a book of hope. We have more common ground than we realize, Hessan says, and we can claim it."

—**Donna Brazile,** veteran political strategist, campaign manager, and Fox News contributor

"Diane Hessan's informative, nuanced new book could not come at a more important time. We have become a deeply divided nation, with mistrust between groups of individuals from different backgrounds and political persuasion growing every day. Hessan has tried to reach beyond these divides by understanding what values Americans hold in common. Interviewing 1,000 people and following up on a weekly basis with 500, she discovered that common ground exists even on hot-button issues like immigration—but it takes listening to those with whom we think we disagree to find those areas on which we actually agree. Readers on both sides of the political divide will benefit from reading this book."

—**Linda Chavez,** director of public liaison,
Reagan White House

"Diane Hessan gets it right by actually staying with her interview respondents over years—seeing them as people, rather than as hit-and-run anonymous data points. By appreciating the unfolding confluence of politics, perspectives, and personalities across a large cross-section of American voters, she charted the disruptive effect over years of how political speech is digested by everyday citizens. With plainspoken but brilliant objective analysis of everyday voters, she fills the niche of in-depth insight once filled by: Eric Hoffer, Studs Terkel, Gail Sheehy, and Mike Barnicle."

—**Jeffrey Sonnenfeld,** senior associate
dean and Lester Crown professor of the practice,
Yale School of Management

"Diane Hessan assembles a remarkable wealth of evidence about why facts alone won't heal American divides, and how listening to other people's perception of what's behind the facts just might bring us together with mutual respect. She examines the Trump years through the eyes of voters on all sides to show that 'we' are both 'us' and 'them.' Her fascinating anecdotes and powerful analysis make for a compelling must-read."

—**Rosabeth Moss Kanter,** professor,
Harvard Business School; bestselling author
of *Confidence* and *Think Outside the Building*

"Diane Hessan has her finger on America's pulse. *Our Common Ground* is a revealing and riveting trip through the psyche of America. Hessan's listening to Americans demonstrates the need for all of us to improve our own listening skills if we are to rediscover the common ground that is essential for democracy to function."

—**Tom Wheeler,** former chairman, Federal
Communications Commission; author of *From
Gutenberg to Google: The History of Our Future*

"Diane Hessan pioneered a new form of research in the corporate world, based around ongoing in-depth discussion with communities of people. It has come to be seen as a necessary and invaluable tool for researchers around the world. Applying that same approach to politics and people's values has resulted in a fascinating book that should be read by anyone interested in America's future."

—**Eric Salama,** senior fellow, Harvard
Kennedy School; former CEO, Kantar Group

"From her unique vantage point, Diane Hessan paints a picture of a nation deeply divided by politics, but not as polarized as one might fear. Drawing on thousands of conversations with American voters over the last four years, Diane offers a simple response to those with whom we differ: 'Tell me more.' Her work is motivated by a deep sense of concern and patriotism, and she offers not only a clear-eyed and comprehensive diagnosis of what ails the body politic but also a suggested treatment. Diane Hessan shows us that our common ground crosses the partisan divide, and gives us hope that this country can rediscover its united purpose—if only we will listen."

—Ambassador Alan Solomont, dean of
the Tisch College of Civic Life, Tufts University

"Diane Hessan is an astute observer of the electorate and its idio-syncrasies. She focuses on our commonalities and our differences to show that if the electorate would concentrate on areas of agreement, we could achieve much more. This is a must-read for the middle 80 percent of the electorate."

—Andrew H. Tisch, co-founder, No Labels

"America remains in the throes of the most divisive political crisis in at least 100 years. How we get past this is what Hessan's thousands of hours of expert listening may help us achieve. Her advice could well have been an alternative title for her book: Tell Me More. This book is a phenomenal guidepost for understanding what is really going on in the US, and a prerequisite for moving to a better future."

—Steven Koltai, senior fellow, Brookings Institution

Our Common Ground

Insights
from Four Years
of Listening to
American Voters

Our
Common
Ground

DIANE HESSAN

RealClear
Publishing

realclearpublishing.com

Our Common Ground
Insights from Four Years of Listening to American Voters

For more information, please contact:
RealClear Publishing
620 Herndon Parkway #320
Herndon, VA 20170
info@realclearpublishing.com

CPSIA Code: PRFRE0521A
Library of Congress Control Number: 2021907748
ISBN-13: 978-1-63755-028-1

Printed in Canada

Contents

The State of Our Disunion

"Give me a call if you can," the email read. It was from Gary, a Republican from Pennsylvania and one of 500 American voters who were participating in my research project. He continued, "I had a terrible day yesterday, and I think I have lost a lot of friends."

I called Gary right away. He was a pretty even-keeled man, 52 years old, a store manager, married with three children—and it was unlike him to exaggerate.

"Hi, Gary. So tell me."

"Well, I went to Capitol Hill to protest yesterday, and now everyone is calling me a terrorist."

I was flabbergasted. It was January 7, 2021, and I couldn't imagine that Gary, a cheerful family man, was one of the people I saw storming the Capitol the previous day.

As he spoke, I learned that Gary and his friends had just driven to Washington, DC, to march. They planned to walk peacefully down Pennsylvania Avenue to express their chagrin about the election of

Joe Biden and what they saw as the radical policies that Democrats were promoting. His sign read, "Honk if you think Socialism Sucks."

"I mean, my wife went to the Women's March in DC back in January of 2017, and everyone thought she was a hero. She had a blast. I just figured I could do the same kind of thing, and I wasn't near that group at the Capitol. Meanwhile, my neighbor called me un-American, and my children are refusing to talk to me."

I asked Gary about the friends who had accompanied him. They were all bowling buddies who didn't like President Trump's values, but who believed that he would do the best job on the economy, their number one issue. "We had nothing to do with those crazy people at the Capitol, but if you watch the news, I was there with my automatic rifle, invading Nancy Pelosi's office. What a mess—and no one wants to hear my truth."

It was not the time for me to tell Gary that Joe Biden was not a socialist. But as we talked, I realized that inaccurate perceptions were behind most of what he was experiencing. He perceived that President Biden would take his hard-earned income, raise his taxes, and use his money to give Americans everything they wanted for free. And his neighbor and his children assumed he was an anarchist just for having been in DC on that day.

I have had thousands of these conversations since 2016 as part of a massive longitudinal study of 500 American voters—conversations about everything from immigration to climate change to mask-wearing to Trump's rallies. Each week, voters from all states, all ages, all ethnicities, and all ends of the political spectrum have shared with me their lives, their dreams, their fears, and their politics. I wrote more than fifty opinion pieces for the *Boston Globe* about what I learned from them, many of which are in this book. And, I have seen over and over again that the assumptions we make about each other—our attitudes, our values, and our rigidity—are horribly inaccurate.

And here's the thing: our inability to hear each other, our specu-
lation, and our impatience are tearing us apart. This has now caused
a crisis in Gary's close circle, and, repeated everywhere in America, it
is dividing us as a country. It's a sickness that permeates the American culture, erodes our collective mental health, paralyzes our ability
to move forward, and makes us hate each other. Substance abuse is
up, mental illness is on the rise, and sales of guns and ammunition
are exploding.

Addressing this problem doesn't require us to agree on everything.
But to turn down the heat, we need to stop presuming, to listen, to
try to understand, to treat each other with dignity, and to know that
most Americans are not crazy radicals. If we can find our common
ground, we can have a much better world.

Common Ground

There is actually much more common ground than you would think
in our country, especially when it comes to policy. Common ground
means just that: the path forward might not be ideal, but it's a good
compromise, a positive step. Let's take immigration as an example.

Most Democrats tell me that Trump supporters want to halt all
immigration into the United States—that they want to build a big
and expensive wall across the entire southern border of the country,
that they want to evict Dreamers, and that they believe that Trump's
separation of children from their parents at the border was a sad but
necessary step.

Most Republicans tell me that Democrats want open borders
where illegal immigrants can pour into our country at their conve-
nience. Once in, they should be able to get a driver's license and free
health care, independent of whether they plan to work or pay taxes.

To be sure, there are Democrats and Republicans who are
proponents of those views, but my research says they are on the

fringes. Only 2 percent of the voters in my sample thought it was okay to separate children and parents, and only a few Democrats were for open borders.

The reality is that most Americans would be fine with an immigration bill that was a compromise: funding a wall in select parts of the border with Mexico, creating a path to citizenship for Dreamers, accelerating citizenship for university students in STEM fields, and stiffening security at the border to discourage further illegal immigration. More specifically, when I laid out the main elements of the proposed Immigration Reform Bill of 2013, more than 80 percent of my voters said they would support the bill. That bill actually passed the Senate and was championed by everyone from Republican Senator Lindsey Graham to Democratic Senator Chuck Schumer. The House never acted on it.

In the meantime, we assume we are far apart on the issue, but it is not the case.

As with immigration, there is also common ground in our country on gun control, health care, infrastructure, climate change, and many other issues. We think we agree on nothing, but it's all perception.

With so much common ground, you would think we'd have significant legislative progress in Washington. The system, however, works against that: if representatives want to get reelected, they are actually better off with popular issues unresolved. It's easier and more powerful to be a Republican candidate and yell to your constituents that immigrants are dangerous people and that, as your voters' ambassador, you will never let those open-border Democrats get their way. It's more compelling to be a Democratic candidate and holler about children at the border and the outrageous cost of a wall, reassuring citizens in your district that you will work every day to make sure the other side doesn't get its way. Resolving the issue takes away valuable talking points. As Kathy, an independent from Ohio, told me, "I used to listen to my congressman for information and for comfort, but now, every time I hear him, he makes me more anxious." Immigrants are worse than you think, liberal teachers brainwash our children, gun owners want to shoot you, minorities are replacing you at work, and you are getting the short end of the stick. Vote for me and I will fix it all.

Our media also plays a role in our divisiveness by amplifying the extreme messages. Cable TV channels get more eyeballs showing white nationalists than they do showing normal people trying to live their everyday lives. So we see the stories of people who believe in extreme policies and we project those stories onto our views of others. "I used to think Republicans were reasonable Americans who just wanted less government interference in our lives," said Matthew, a Democrat from Florida. "But I have been watching MSNBC and it has convinced me not to spend a lot of time with my Republican friends anymore." Turn on the news and it is all discord all the time: we hear regularly about our divided America, that constant case of us versus them, the Never-Trumpers versus the Lock-Her-Uppers, the Elites versus the Deplorables. The fringes are clearly getting the airtime. Those media clips get shared on Facebook and Twitter, which keeps conservatives in their own information bubble and liberals in a separate bubble.

The more we watch, the more we read, the more apprehensive we become. It feels better to blame the other guys and to parrot back a story you heard—even if it's extreme. At this point, if you ask most Republicans about the Democratic Party, they will say Democrats are a bunch of elitist socialists who want to take my hard-earned tax dollars and give them away to illegal immigrants, criminals, and people who are too lazy to work. And who want to take away guns, allow women to use abortions as birth control, and, more recently, to completely dismantle policing. Or, if you ask most Democrats about Trump supporters, they will say that they are a bunch of hypocritical, uneducated deplorables, who sleep with their guns, refuse to wear masks, deny that climate change is happening, and never met a Black person they liked. Both of these views are inaccurate, but these are the stereotypes that were on the ballot in 2020, and they dominate our perspectives.

Voting Against Versus Voting For

"I always thought of myself as a Democrat," said Joseph, a Republican from Texas. "I thought that the Dems were cool and young and always trying something new, breaking the mold, putting money in your pocket, looking out for the people, and slamming the rich corporations." Then, he told me, things changed. "Our senators explained that the Dems were actually taking my tax money and funding people who are not out there earning their living. I heard a news story about someone on welfare who didn't want to work because it was easier to get a government handout. And I also noticed that Fox News was talking nonstop about the economy, and CNN was talking nonstop about sexual orientation. I am all for letting transgender people pick whatever bathroom they want, but I don't want to hear about it as the main issue for our country. So I guess I am voting against the Dems these days rather than for the Republicans."

This theme dominates the discussions I have with voters. They voted against someone rather than supporting their candidate because of horror stories about the other side. "I don't like Trump, but the alternative is much worse" was a frequent cry from those who supported him.

In 2016, one of the primary reasons that people voted for Donald Trump was not that they thought he was a really great guy. They just hated Hillary Clinton. Trump supporters reported to me that she was totally corrupt and listed an entire lifetime of questionable activities: Whitewater, Vince Foster, the Clinton Foundation, Benghazi, and "stealing furniture from the White House on their way out." Although each of these issues was resolved in Hillary Clinton's favor, voters were not appeased. "Normal law-abiding, ethical people just don't have all of those shady, questionable things in their lives," said Susan, a Republican from North Carolina. Women told me that Clinton was a hypocrite to say that she was a supporter of women, when she had once defended her husband against women who accused him of sexual harassment. And the famous emails, rather than being a pivotal factor in their decision to vote for Trump, were just one more thing to pile onto their list.

Of course, that same year, many voters chose Hillary Clinton because they hated Donald Trump, calling out his criticism of Gold Star families, his conversation with Billy Bush about his sexual escapades, his narcissism, his name-calling, his track record of business failures, his mocking of a disabled reporter, and more.

This "dislike of the alternative" also happened in 2020. Over half of my voters who chose Biden told me they were just voting against Trump. And over half of those who voted for Trump told me they were just voting against Biden.

Trump supporters saw a strong man who tells it like it is, works hard, loves his family, and made huge progress despite unprecedented lawsuits, hearings, and general obstruction from the other party—the likes of which had never been seen before. They think Biden has dementia, will be hijacked by the "radical liberals" in the party and mess up any chance of an economic recovery, and is just too quiet and weak for our times.

Biden supporters saw an experienced, empathetic man who will unite our country, bring sanity back to the White House, build a great and expert team, and watch out for the little guy—especially because of his background. They saw Trump as a lying, cheating buffoon who panders to Putin and cares only about himself.

The Voter Fraud Question

After winning the 2016 presidential election but losing the popular vote, President Trump claimed that he actually won the popular vote if you eliminated all of the illegal votes for Hillary Clinton. This narrative continued throughout his 2020 presidential campaign, as he convinced his supporters that the only way a tired 78-year-old Joe Biden could win was through mass numbers of illegal ballots cast by enemies on the Democratic side. His supporters and the media amplified this message, and by the time Trump lost, he had convinced millions of Americans that it was all because of fraud.

My data says that about half of those who voted for Trump believe he lost the election, and the other half believe that there was significant fraud and that Trump most likely won. This has been reinforced by popular networks like Newsmax and One America News Network (OAN); when Fox News reported no voter fraud, they lost millions of viewers, and thus significant market share, to more pro-Trump networks. Projecting my data to the population as a whole would mean that there are more than 30 million Americans who see Biden as an illegitimate president. Although most of these people would never storm the Capitol, they are unhappy with the outcome and feel dismissed and ignored.

Said Brenda from Pennsylvania, "I sincerely believe this election was stolen. There is no way someone as demented as Biden could have won legitimately, not to mention the blatant proof via videos and sworn affidavits from countless witnesses."

Even more important, most Republicans who believe Trump lost are fine with the continued claims of fraud because they see it as tit for tat. In January of 2017, they watched "500,000 women with pussy hats" converge on Washington, DC. Although most of the women went to express support for gender equality, affordable care, reproductive freedom, and other issues that they thought would lack support in a Trump administration, the conservative media told a different story: the march was a dangerous anti-Trump protest. Women carried signs that read, "Not My President," a rejection of a duly elected candidate by the other party. Thus, Republicans see the resistance to the 2020 election result as similar, just in reverse. "Now you Democrats know how it feels," said Brent from Oklahoma.

The Case for Conversation

We are inexorably divided in our country because of what we have come to believe about the other side. The extremes get the megaphone, both among our political leaders and in the media, and this in turn creates our extreme perceptions. The algorithms created by our social networks fuel the fire even more. The result is a narrative that people from the other party are crazy, selfish, and focused on the wrong issues. Nobody likes it this way: 483 of my 500 voters tell me they are distressed about the disunity.

Many Americans believe that those in the other party are dangerous. Like our president, we have resorted to calling people names: deplorables, low-information voters, elitists, socialists, fascists, radicals, racists, Nazis, idiots. We make assumptions about their values, and we don't trust them. We believe that the other party as we knew it is dead. And we are afraid of what they will do if their candidate doesn't win. It's a civil war, conducted in our minds and documented on platforms like Facebook.

My voters tell me that they expect violence in the future, instigated by the other party. Sales of small, concealable guns and AR-15s are at record highs, and the demand for ammunition is tantamount to the run on toilet paper early in the COVID pandemic.[1]

We need to put a halt to the insanity.

It's clear that promises by President Biden to unite our country will not be enough. We could hope that the media changes—that they realize the enormous responsibility they have in shaping public perception and that they commit to being far less inflammatory and less tolerant of on-air conspiracy-mongering. We could hope that bridge groups like The Lincoln Project or No Labels use their communication skills to try to bring us together. We could hope that our state governors can band together to model what harmony and public safety can look like. Or we could hope for urgent messages and actions by our representatives in Congress about how hating each other is fruitless. These hopes may be overly optimistic, but they're more likely than what some imagine: that we will pull together as a country because the guys on the other side suddenly realize that they are wrong.

Telling someone who believes there was fraud that they are just wrong doesn't work. Explaining to that person that judges threw out 60 of 61 lawsuits claiming fraud doesn't work either, because it is counter to everything they have come to believe about the world.

And similarly, telling someone who hates Donald Trump that he has been a great president is fruitless. Sending that person a long list of Trump's accomplishments doesn't work either, because it is counter to everything they have come to believe about the world.

The only solution is listening. Instead of lecturing the other side—sending them articles and lists and videos to prove they are uninformed—dialogue *actually works*. We have seen it over the years: groups of Republican and Democratic voters sitting in a room, talking for a day, and leaving with more understanding of each other; people with different views agreeing to listen hard to each other and try to walk in each other's shoes. When this happens, the temperature goes down. When people are treated with dignity, when they feel that their perspective matters, they are eventually much better at listening to your facts.

Conversation is less about coming to agreement than about honoring the other person's perspective. It's taking a deep breath and making the assumption that the person on the other side might share values with you after all.

A great example of this happened in July of 2020, when Philadelphia Eagles wide receiver DeSean Jackson posted an anti-Semitic post on Twitter. Although a storm of criticism followed, Julian Edelman of the New England Patriots, who is Jewish, reached out to Jackson to ask for a conversation about why he posted the quote. Edelman wanted to take Jackson to the Holocaust Memorial Museum, but he also wanted Jackson to take him to the National Museum of African American History and Culture. The two had a conversation about challenges for Blacks and Jews that they kept private, and they made museum plans for after the football season. This was all about looking for common ground, instead of accusing and blaming.

Listening doesn't take a sophisticated set of skills. Most of the time, it is about learning to use three words: Tell me more.

You are afraid that a minority will take your job? Tell me more.

You are afraid that your guns will be taken away from you? Tell me more.

You think it's okay for Donald Trump to lie? Tell me more.

You think it's okay for the federal government to increase your taxes? Tell me more.

The result is often surprising. Instead of feeling outraged, we ask more questions and we start to learn how a regular person could feel the way they do.

Listen to people who dismiss Trump's lies and learn they are convinced that all politicians lie—and that they have dozens of examples.

Listen to people who think eliminating student loan debt is a terrible idea and learn the story of how they paid off the loans of their three children by working two jobs for eleven years.

Listen to the people who came to the United States illegally and learn the story of how they escaped unimaginable conditions and couldn't wait for legal entry.

Listen to a person who has a large gun collection and learn that it's the same to them as somebody else's precious baseball card collection.

If we could get a critical mass of Americans to listen hard—and to consider that what they assume about others just might be wrong—it could transform our country. We could stop the paralysis in Washington, we could turn down the heat, and we could get so much done.

If you are up for the journey, this book will get you started. It will help you understand why people love Trump's rallies, why voters don't care about cozying up to Vladimir Putin, why most Republicans think Democrats are radical socialists, and how our attitudes play out across the issues of the day. It will tell you why Democratic Congresswoman Ilhan Omar and Republican Congresswoman Marjorie Taylor Greene are symbols of the same problems. And, if you are up for taking a deep breath and having a dialogue with someone you think you can't tolerate, you will get some guidance for how to get started.

Here is what I know: we are not merely Black or White, Democrat or Republican, rich or poor, Southern or Northern. We are complicated, flawed human beings who are not always rational—and we are trying to move forward in life in the best way we can. Along the way, we pick up beliefs and influences that shape who we are. If we choose to judge each other solely by a box that we checked, we are missing the story. We are missing humanity.

Part I

How Pivotal Events Fuel Our Discord

When I speak with voters about our country, it reminds me that most Americans are not glued to the television, waiting for the outcome of a House vote or anticipating the next White House press briefing. They are living their lives, inattentive to politics. This all changes, however, at consequential moments: a crisis, a scandal, a march, or some other pivotal event. Suddenly people engage, bringing to light the assumptions, perceptions, and values that have created fault lines in our electorate.

In this section, I review my findings about those pivotal events, which are still relevant today. Many of them are about race, including the white supremacy march in Charlottesville, the NFL players taking a knee during the national anthem, and Trump's vicious attack on the four congresswomen of color who made up the liberal "Squad."

But the same divisions emerge from other cases: the nomination of Brett Kavanaugh to the Supreme Court, the withdrawal from the Iran nuclear deal, the first presidential debate of 2020, and the terrifying siege on Capitol Hill of January 2021.

If you wanted to see where the nation was going over those years, there was no better diagnostic than the 2017 special election in Alabama, which pitted liberal Democrat Doug Jones against Roy Moore, a conservative Republican accused of pedophile sexual behavior. Conservative voters in my panel refused to believe the accusations, and many planned to vote for Moore anyway. While Jones eked out a victory, the state switched back to a conservative Republican in the 2020 election. Could the same thing happen in the nation as a whole?

There is precious little unity in these events, and many of them are still front and center, such as the claims of voter fraud in our elections. If we are to once again learn to listen to each other, that listening must start by understanding the differences in perspective that these columns illuminate.

The Moment Voters Shifted to Trump

The 2016 election of Donald Trump marked a turning point in American politics. Because Trump was far behind Hillary Clinton in polls, much of the nation found itself in shock, waking up on the day after the election to a result they never expected: a nonpolitician who was a reality TV star and who defied political norms would be the next leader of the United States. Among the voters on my panel, more than 90 percent told me they were surprised at the election outcome. A year later, people could still remember where they were and what they were wearing when they heard the news.

In the five months before the election, I volunteered to conduct a research project for the Clinton campaign to understand undecided voters in swing states. I recruited, interviewed, and tracked 300 voters on a weekly basis to see how they were leaning and why, looking for shifts in their sentiments. Most pundits suggested that undecided voters were swayed to vote for Trump on October 28 when FBI Director James Comey sent a letter to Congress about the existence of new emails that were "pertinent to the investigation." I found something different.

In my data, the moment when undecided voters shifted was in September, when Hillary Clinton referred to half of Trump voters as being in a "basket of deplorables." In the 24 hours following that statement, I received more unsolicited and emotional comments from my voter panel than I did on any other day of the study. With this statement, Clinton had alienated a large class of undecided voters. Two weeks after the election, I wrote about this point in an op-ed for the *Boston Globe*, reprinted below. During an election postmortem at the Kennedy School of Government at Harvard University, Jake Tapper of CNN quoted my article and asked campaign managers Robby Mook and Kellyanne Conway about my data[1]—and my column went viral.

During this process, I also learned how challenging it is to tell the truth to people who do not want to hear it. The people who commented online about the piece seemed more interested in scoring points against the other side than in understanding what was happening. Any positive voter sentiment I quoted about Trump caused liberals to respond with anger, while the reverse was true for any positive quotes about Clinton.

Understanding the Undecided Voters
November 21, 2016[2]

When I was growing up outside of Philadelphia in the '60s, a friend lived in Wilkes-Barre, Pennsylvania, and so I was excited this past July to be on the phone with George, a 58-year-old Democrat from the same town, who was undecided about which presidential candidate would get his vote on November 8.

George was one of the many "friends" I made over the last four months, while working on special assignment for the Clinton campaign. My task was to help her campaign understand undecided voters in swing states. Finding them and getting insights from them was right up my alley—a skill I honed over my 14 years as CEO of C Space—and when I got a call to help, I couldn't resist. I left my job as CEO of Startup Institute, and was off and running.

At first, I couldn't understand how anyone could be undecided. The distinction between Donald Trump and Hillary Clinton was so clear to me, the gap so wide. Much to my surprise, it was easy to find the undecideds: people who had significant enough reservations about both candidates that they were searching for a sign, looking for more information, or just waiting it out until November.

Over the summer, I found and interviewed over 300 undecided voters, and 250 of them agreed to stay in touch, to send me weekly diary entries about their emotions, what they were thinking about both Clinton and Trump, and how they were leaning when it came to their vote. I had no responsibility to change their views; instead, I synthesized the data that I was collecting, and reported in to the campaign. I also added the insights that I had and made regular suggestions about how the campaign might better articulate its positions and modify its strategies.

When George and I spoke, I told him I had been in his town several times, and he told me how the Miners Bank building had been turned into luxury condos. "Nice, but not for me and my neighbors," he added.

George's story was one I ultimately heard over and over: he had lived in that part of Pennsylvania his entire life, had worked hard, raised a family, paid his debts, sacrificed to get his kids through Wilkes University, and tried to do the right thing for others. "The government never helped me, but I was okay with that," he said. "I made mistakes, had some scary moments, and my wife worked also at the local library to help out. I paid my bills, including my doctor bills.

"Now I see my tax dollars going to handouts for others who don't want to work as hard as I did, and I can't afford my health care. Everyone is being taken care of but me. I feel left out, and it makes me feel that I want my country back."

All through the summer and into the fall, George was undecided. Clinton was a Democrat, and Democrats historically helped the working class—but Trump painted a new picture.

As time went on, George was more and more disgusted. "All I know is that I am going to hold my nose when I walk into that voting booth," he said. "Trump is a loose cannon who arrived on third base at birth—and I have never trusted the Clintons, from Whitewater to the Foundation."

Listening to all of the undecideds, I thought that there was still hope for the Clinton team.

In July and August, many interesting themes popped up. For instance, early on, I learned that the attraction of Trump was that he was a successful businessman. People did wonder about how successful he really was, and I wrote a piece to the campaign about Trump and his tax returns. Voters didn't care whether he paid taxes or not—and thought he was smart to pay none. But they thought Trump's returns could show whether he was charitable (important) and whether he was as rich as he claimed he was (more important).

In September, more themes arose. The undecided voters didn't really believe Clinton had health problems, and most didn't believe that Trump was a racist. They were sure that Clinton cared more about climate change (which they mostly also cared about), and that Trump would never get Mexico to pay for the wall. And they weren't worried that Trump didn't know what was going on in Crimea, because they didn't either.

During the debates, I tracked what was compelling and reported in. They liked it when Clinton was calm and not shouting. They were bombarded by NRA ads that claimed Clinton would take away their guns. It bothered them that Trump was a bully and was outrageous in his insensitivity to people with disabilities. It bothered them that someone on Clinton's staff literally took a hammer and smashed her Blackberries. On the other hand, Bernie Sanders was right: my voters were sick of hearing about emails.

Last week, I reread all of my notes. There was one moment when I saw more undecided voters shift to Trump than any other, when it all changed, when voters began to speak differently about their choice. It wasn't FBI Director James Comey, Part One or Part Two; it wasn't Benghazi or the emails or Bill Clinton's visit with Attorney General Loretta Lynch on the tarmac. No, the conversation shifted the most during the weekend of September 9, after Clinton said, "You can put half of Trump supporters into what I call the basket of deplorables."

All hell broke loose.

George told me that his neighborhood was outraged, that many of his hard-working, churchgoing, family-loving friends resented being called that name. He told me that he looked up the word in the dictionary, and that it meant something so bad that there is no hope, like the aftermath of a tsunami. You know, he said, Clinton ended up being the biggest bully of them all. Whereas Trump bullied her, she bullied Wilkes-Barre.

Things were not the same after that, at least with my voters. I remember wondering whether that moment was like Romney's 47 percent: a comment during a fund-raiser from which the candidate would never recover, proof that, like Romney, Clinton was an out-of-touch rich person who didn't really get it. It struck me that many of the people who were considering Trump were just hard-working Americans who wanted better odds for a good life.

George stuck with his weekly diaries until the very end. He went to two rallies: a passionate event with 500 attendees honoring Joe Biden—"I like him, but he is not running"— and a rally on October 15 for Trump, along with 10,000 other neighbors. He told me that the Trump rally was "the most fun I have had in years. Trump would say, 'What am I going to build?' And we would scream, 'A wall!' He would say, 'And who is going to pay for it?' We yelled back, 'Mexico!' He thought we were smart and he didn't talk above us. We know that he's not actually going to get Mexico to pay for it, but it was fun to lighten up, to cheer along with everyone else, just like back in high school, when we would cheer that our teams were definitely going to win, even when they were bad."

I heard this from scores of undecided voters in swing states. They didn't like either candidate. They just wanted to be understood. At the end of the day, they cared less about Trump's temperament and more about whether he "got" them. They were smart, they knew the cheers, Trump gave them a voice, and he certainly didn't think they were deplorable. I didn't hear this from everyone, but it was striking to read the comments of voters who were struggling to make a decision, and who went with the candidate who made them feel important. It might have been enough to make 70 electoral votes' worth of difference.

It is crushing to me that Clinton lost. When my mother was dying, in 2014, she told me that her only regret was that she never saw a woman president. I wanted to see one, and Clinton was my big chance: a smart, committed, experienced woman who would be trusted to deal with the most serious of crises. I could taste her victory: even with her flaws, she was running against a misogynistic, racist, inexperienced birther.

George voted for Trump. He told me it was a difficult decision, but that he is optimistic that it will be fine. He told me he hopes that I go to Washington on January 21 to send Trump a message that women and minorities still count. I will be there with my daughters, hoping that my new president will try hard to understand me.

So, where do we go from here? I don't know the full answer, but my recent experience does help me know where to start. Whether you liked Clinton or not, we can probably all agree that we are Stronger Together—and I have learned that instead of speaking about each other, we need to speak with each other. If you had asked me to describe a Trump voter last spring, I would have been largely wrong about their motivations, dreams, and even their values. Sure, there are extremists among them, but it was eye opening to realize how legitimate the concerns of many are, and to realize that, if I just listened hard, I would find that I have more in common with the Georges of the world than I could ever have imagined. Empathy—trying to understand others as deeply as possible—is an important first step, whether around the Thanksgiving table or in social media. President Obama said it eloquently last week, noting that our election is ultimately an intramural scrimmage because we are all on one team. If we believe in liberty and justice for all, we have to acknowledge how terrible it is to feel left out—and then to ask questions, learn, and walk in each other's shoes.

The Protest in Charlottesville Results in Fury—on Both Sides

In August of 2018 we witnessed the Unite the Right rally, organized to protest the removal of Confederate monuments, on the streets of Charlottesville, Virginia. The rally attracted a variety of white supremacist and neo-Nazi groups, including some who chanted racist and anti-Semitic slogans and carried Nazi and Confederate flags. One admitted white supremacist, James Alex Fields Jr., rammed his car into a crowd of counterprotesters, killing one, Heather Heyer, and injuring nineteen others.

This was President Trump's first chance to make a symbolic gesture regarding racist attitudes. But his statements, which called out hatred and bigotry "on many sides," and later asserted that there were "very fine people on both sides," became a litmus test for voters; progressives saw a dog whistle to the most racist of his white supporters, while Trump supporters perceived a few harmless words that mostly served to enrage liberals. As a result of those statements, Joe Biden says he was inspired to run for president of the United States.

There were only a few acknowledged racists among the Trump supporters in my panel; most were horrified at the violence in Charlottesville. And they were quite emotional about the protests, as well as the subsequent calls to remove Confederate statues.

This incident also presaged the unconditional loyalty of Trump supporters, who continued to back the president despite blistering criticism in the media. The themes I heard from voters about Charlottesville have endured: we hear them in response to controversial events even today.

Trump Voters in the Aftermath of Charlottesville
August 21, 2017[3]

For many Democrats, this has been the worst two weeks of the Trump presidency. In the aftermath of frightening brinksmanship between President Trump and Kim Jong-un of North Korea, attention turned to Charlottesville, and to a president who is unwilling to clearly and directly call out neo-Nazis and white supremacists for their actions. Clinton voters tell me they saw the two things they were most worried about when their candidate lost: a careless and impetuous president creating unstable international relations—and a president who failed to respect the dignity of all Americans.

"The events in Charlottesville have really shaken me, and almost everyone I know," Jennifer, 31, from Connecticut told me. "This can't possibly last another three years, because there is just no one who can defend his behavior at this point." Republicans like Senator Marco Rubio and Congressman Charlie Dent agreed. So did corporate CEOs.

Emotions are high in the United States of America. Just look at social media, or just be old fashioned and turn on the TV.

Meanwhile, the Trump base is in disbelief—not about the president, but about the hysteria. Although they are horrified by the events in Charlottesville, and the murderous nutjob who drove his car through a crowd and killed 32-year-old Heather Heyer, they are incredulous that, once again, the "media and elites" have decided to spend 24/7 trashing Trump over a few words and the order he said them in.

"Concentrating on whether Donald Trump said things the way you would say them is a precious waste of time to me," argued Mitch, 41, from Nebraska. "Every minute that we spend giving a voice to those awful white nationalists is a minute that we don't spend working on increasing good jobs, securing our borders, defeating ISIS, and helping to put food on people's tables."

Charlie, 56, of Georgia, agrees. "We were on the brink of war with a crazy man in North Korea, we have a new issue with Iran, we have big challenges with health care and infrastructure, the opioid crisis is worsening, and we have decided to spend most of our time parsing the president's words. I think it's insane."

Trump voters take offense at the narrative that links them to the white supremacist movement. It goes like this: neo-Nazis are disgusting, and they wouldn't be so bold if Trump were not president, therefore people who support Trump are racists and bigots, so anyone wearing a "Make America Great Again" cap is to blame for all the hatred. Most Trump voters I speak with believe that white supremacist Chris Cantwell is a repugnant, sickening subhuman, and that to imply that he and his clan represent Trump voters is just plain ignorant and insulting. If liberals are not to blame for James Hodgkinson, the deranged radical who shot Republican members of Congress practicing for a baseball game, then why, they say, would you blame Trump voters for a reactionary running people over with a car?

Instead, they see a president delivering on his campaign promises despite the resistance. They send me article after article, video after video, of Trump denouncing the KKK and neo-Nazis, they count the number of Jewish and Black people on the White House staff, and they conclude that calling Trump a racist is a lie intended to distract us from what Trump is doing to help the country.

Says Russell, 77, from California, "The stock market is way up, the economy is starting to really crank, we have 1 million new jobs, housing sales have doubled, companies are getting the message that they will be celebrated if they build in the US, unemployment is at a new low, the borders are significantly more secure, we have a brilliant new Supreme Court justice and a freeze on government hiring. Say that this is not all Trump's doing, fine—but we have so much good news, and also so many huge challenges in our country and world. Why are we giving all of our air time to the lunatics and skinheads who marched in beautiful Charlottesville—and why do we insist on blaming our president for James Alex Fields [the man charged with driving the car into the crowd in Charlottesville] and for those disgusting Nazis?"

Trump voters are not ignoring his words, but the overwhelming majority are not racist demons. They hate the KKK as much as the rest of America. They were desperate for change, and thought Hillary Clinton was, at best, a continuation of the greed and bureaucracy they see in Washington.

They also believe that Trump is not political enough to read a script and walk away. They believe that actions speak louder than words, and they like his actions. Conversely, many of them liked the words of Obama, but felt that his actions left them on the sidelines. As a result, their standards for the role of president are just different. Rather than looking to their leader for moral leadership, they look to him for leadership on growing the economy and on protecting our citizens. They are more likely to shake their heads, state that he is a flawed man, and go elsewhere for moral leadership: their local leaders, their churches, their families.

We can ignore the perspective of these Trump voters, but realistically, we must understand that they exist, there are plenty of them, and they are our fellow Americans. It might feel good to read the recent *New York Times* article by a Trump voter who finally changed his mind, but this is not a signal about a trend—at least from my data. Of the 200 Trump voters I speak with weekly, only four say they would have voted differently.

Outrage, justified as it may be, accomplishes little. Anger and hatred are an addictive cocktail and many of us are drinking it, surrounded by our Facebook friends with similar viewpoints. It's human to feel the anger, and therapeutic to express it with friends, but it would be ideal to do more. A few of the Clinton voters in my research are talking about impeachment. Most agree, however, that although several Republican senators and representatives have complained bitterly about Trump, that doesn't mean they'll vote to get rid of him. While they are waiting around for Robert Mueller to produce a smoking gun, they believe that the country and the government will go on.

Finally, if you're concerned about racial hatred and white supremacy, do something nonviolent to take it on. Donate to the Southern Poverty Law Center (which has identified 917 hate groups in the United States) or the ACLU or the Anti-Defamation League. Go to social media to thank leaders who believe what you do, independent of party. Take Josh Bernoff's pro-bono pledge[4] to dedicate your time and expertise to groups that fight intolerance. It's time to all work together to stop the madness.

Boycott the NFL? Two Views of What It Means to Take a Knee

During the NFL preseason of 2016, San Francisco 49ers quarterback Colin Kaepernick sat and then knelt during the national anthem. Many endorsed Kaepernick's action as a peaceful protest against police brutality and racial inequality, but others criticized it as outrageous and unpatriotic. Several other players copied Kaepernick, whose action became known as "taking a knee," during the 2016 season, but the silent protests escalated in the fall of 2017, especially after Cleveland Browns tight end Seth DeValve became the first white football player to take a knee. On September 24, at a rally, President Trump commented on football players kneeling during the national anthem.[5] "Wouldn't you love to see one of these NFL owners, when someone disrespects our flag, to say, 'Get that son of a bitch off the field right now'? Out. He's fired. He's fired." Trump, in his own way, called for a boycott, adding, "But do you know what's hurting the game more…? When people like yourselves turn on the television and you see those players taking the knee when they're playing our great national anthem. The only thing you could do better is if you see it, even if it's one player, leave the stadium. I guarantee things will stop. Things will stop. Just pick up and leave. Pick up and leave." The following weekend, more than 200 NFL players and coaches either sat or took a knee when "The Star-Spangled Banner" was played.

Once again in this incident, symbols electrified and divided voters. As I spoke with voters, it became clear that what was peaceful for one side was disrespectful for the other. Trump's ability to stoke the flames about this particular controversy was a significant distraction from a series of crises at the time: significant tensions in the relationship between the US and North Korea, and hurricanes in Houston, Puerto Rico, and Florida. The formula—pick an issue all Americans can understand, find a controversial angle, and use it to divert people's attention—works, especially when it is spread via every means, from social media to Russian bots. It fuels our divide, and we all take the bait.

Why Trump Voters Want to Boycott the NFL

September 28, 2017 [6]

Along with yoga and power naps, most Americans believe that a perfect way to escape from the stress of our daily lives is to sit back and watch a ballgame. That all changed this past week.

Our country is stressed over President Trump's fight with the NFL, which started as an off-the-cuff statement at an Alabama rally and ballooned into one more week of divisiveness between those who support Trump and those who don't.

The progressives I have interviewed are appalled at Trump's SOB comments, his insistence on criticizing a peaceful demonstration of free speech, and as some believe, his racism. Steve Kerr, the head coach of the Golden State Warriors, made an impassioned plea, in *Sports Illustrated*,[7] for the president to bring us together and not divide us.

However, among the 400 voters participating in my research since last December, more than 40 percent are supporting the president. Many are calling for a boycott of the NFL this weekend, and it's important to understand why. Among these voters, there are four reasons.

The first is patriotism: the flag is a sacred symbol of pride and unity. Deborah from New Hampshire said, "Saluting the flag and singing the national anthem is dignified, expected, comforting, and entrenched in routine, and it obviously demonstrates respect for our country. It's a feel-good moment for most people and very important for our children to experience."

People like Deborah want our president to be outraged about those who disrespect the flag. They used words like "despicable" and "a disgrace" to describe the Ravens/Jaguars game in London, where players took a knee for the national anthem and stood for "God Save the Queen." In their eyes, football players and coaches made a mockery of our nation.

The second reason is the NFL leaders' hypocrisy. Trump supporters question why the NFL didn't step in and prevent the problem in advance. They cite the case from July of 2017, when Dallas Cowboys tight end Jason Witten suggested wearing a helmet decal in support of Dallas police, after five officers were shot dead by a man who claimed he wanted to kill white people. The team wore the decals during practice, but the NFL rejected the team's petition to wear the stickers during regular games. The NFL has also cited league rules in banning one player's request to wear green shoes in support of mental health issues. If these displays are banned, they ask, why shouldn't the NFL ban protests during the national anthem?

Thirdly, they feel liberals celebrate free speech, but not when it's conservatives who are speaking. Tom from Wyoming said, "Liberals are all in support of free speech when it is on their own terms, like football players kneeling, but then they want to keep Milo Yiannopoulos from speaking at Berkeley. I am just left shaking my head at everyone from both parties."

Finally, they want players to be more responsible in how they protest injustice. "Why didn't the players scream in protest against domestic violence when Ray Rice sucker-punched his girlfriend so hard that she lost consciousness for 30 minutes?" asked Ron from West Virginia. And rather than taking actions that divide the country and don't accomplish much for those they are trying to help, people on Main Street want to see more genuine altruism from athletes. Kate from South Carolina said, "They could all make such a big difference. Maybe if they quit the knee B.S. and actually took the time to help some of those individuals who are so oppressed." Added Sarah from Connecticut, "How about pouring some of that money back into the places they came from to make them better? Or take a stand against the gangs who are making our communities unsafe?" When I mentioned to Kate and Sarah that many NFL athletes spend significant time giving back to their communities, they responded that for all but a few players, these actions are just for appearances, and not truly impactful. They insist that millionaire football players have joined the elite and no longer can relate to middle America.

The people who support Trump are not uniformly in favor of how he has behaved over the past week. They acknowledge the immaturity in his words, his unfortunate tweets, and his own inconsistencies, but they support his overall message about the flag and believe that people who dislike the president will find fault with anything that he says. Tom from Wyoming noted, "I feel in my heart that all Americans share a love for the country, but some folks are simply not going to allow Trump to lead under any circumstances."

Why did Trump even take us here? As a distraction from the other issues he's dealing with, it's ultimately ineffective. No one has forgotten about North Korea, health care, or hurricanes. More likely, Trump is doing what he has done for the last two years: forcing the Democrats yet again into a losing game of identity politics. Here the sense of community we get from Sunday football-watching diminishes, as people are more interested in who wins the take-the-knee competition than whether our team wins. In this game, everyone fights for their corner of the world instead of listening, asking, and learning from each other—preventing us from dealing with the complex issues facing our country.

The Spectacle of the Alabama Special Election

The special election in December of 2017 to fill a Senate seat in Alabama was a revealing test case for attitudes in this country. Former prosecutor Doug Jones, a Democrat, faced off against Roy Moore, the Republican former chief justice of the Alabama Supreme Court and a staunch conservative. In any ordinary election in the Deep South, Moore would be a shoo-in. But after Moore was accused of sexual misconduct with a 14-year-old girl, along with other creepy behavior, the election became a national news story for weeks, with a more complex set of moral choices.

As I found from my interviews with Alabamians, support for a candidate does not necessarily shift in the face of scandalous accusations. Although news organizations like the *Washington Post* presented compelling proof of assault from several women, many of my voters were unwilling to believe that Moore was guilty, especially when the candidate himself condemned the allegations. This led me to predict (wrongly) that Moore would win. As it turned out, enough disgusted Republicans stayed home and enough energized Democrats turned out to propel Jones to a narrow win, making him the first Democrat elected statewide in Alabama in 25 years. Faithful Republicans, unhappy with the Jones victory, vowed that he would be a one-term senator—and when Senator Jones voted no on the appointment of Brett Kavanaugh to the Supreme Court, conservative Alabama voters had just the ammunition they needed. In the 2020 election, Jones was widely viewed as the most vulnerable of any incumbent senator; he lost his reelection campaign in 2020 to the Republican Tommy Tuberville, a former football coach that Trump had endorsed.

Even so, this election reflected the views of the country. In Alabama, as in the nation as a whole, Republican voters proved resistant to claims of misconduct about a candidate who shared their values. But in the special election in Alabama, enough Republicans deserted the scandal-tainted Moore to cause him to lose the election—just as in the 2020 presidential election, conservative and moderate defectors, fed up with Trump's behavior, cost him the election. (Moore also pursued fruitless claims of voter fraud after losing, just as Trump would three years later.)

Will the nation turn back to Republicans in 2022 and 2024, just as Alabama voters returned to Tuberville? As I write this, it's hard to say, but anyone who counts Republicans out hasn't accounted for how quickly Alabama flipped back to red once an accused pedophile was no longer on the ballot.

The View from Alabama: Why Roy Moore Will Win

December 7, 2017[8]

On December 12, Alabama voters will elect either Democrat Doug Jones or Republican Roy Moore to the US Senate.

Complicating this race is a report from the *Washington Post*[9] that Roy Moore, a former chief justice of the state Supreme Court, engaged in sexual misconduct with a 14-year-old girl, followed by a string of additional accusations[10] from women about Moore's misconduct. According to the latest polls, the race is neck and neck, which has left voters outside the South wondering what Alabamians could possibly be thinking. So I asked them.

In some ways, this race started as a microcosm of the 2016 presidential election, pitting a Democrat without much of an inspired base against a Republican who, even before the charges were made, was seen as a bizarre man. And as in the national election, some mainstream Republicans have abandoned their candidate. Even before these allegations came out, President Trump had originally supported Moore's primary opponent, Luther Strange. Now Senate majority leader Mitch McConnell admits he believes the women accusers, Republican Senator Jeff Flake is supporting the Democrat, and even Ivanka Trump is going against her father's wishes and condemning the judge. There are lots of controversial issues in our country, but when you come right down to it, it's easy to say you don't like pedophiles.

So why are people in Alabama supporting Moore? Based on my conversations with them, Alabama Republicans, just like you and me, would never vote for a pedophile. But they're not convinced the accusations are true.

Linda voted for Moore in the primary, and intends to vote for him again. "I have read all of the accusations, but there is no smoking gun," she said. "There is no blue dress, no pictures, no verification of handwriting analysis." She reminds me that Moore denies the charges, insisting that they are absolute lies. With no evidence other than stories from 40 years ago, Linda is sticking with her candidate. She has considered that the women accusers are telling the truth, but she also wonders whether they are liberal voters with an agenda who will do anything to keep Moore from getting into office. Added Rick, who lives in rural Alabama, "Show me the evidence. I would never vote for a pedophile, and so I am waiting for more information."

Besides, they ask, what is the alternative? Just as many voters last November cast their ballots against a candidate rather than for one, the same holds in Alabama. In the primary, many voters went with Moore as a vote against Luther Strange, who, as attorney general, refused to investigate a corrupt governor facing both a sexual scandal and accusations about using campaign funds for personal use. They saw Strange as crooked and thus voted for Moore, a judge whose positions, as well as his eccentricities, were familiar. Now the alternative is Doug Jones, a liberal, whom they call "the Hillary Clinton of Alabama." For antiabortion, pro-Second-Amendment, pro-building-a-wall Republicans, Jones is on the wrong side of the issues they care about. Voters won't abandon the opportunity for a conservative Republican solely on hearsay.

If more concrete proof emerged against Moore, would they vote for Jones? Never. They told me that if they were convinced of Moore's guilt, they would just stay home, reducing what is already expected to be very low voter turnout. If Moore is elected and then, subsequently, proof comes out, they fully expect that he will be removed, and that Kay Ivey, the governor of Alabama, will replace him with a better conservative.

If you've read the *Washington Post* article about Moore and teenage girls, you may find this hard to understand. But your idea of the *Post*'s standards is probably different from that of many Alabama voters, who inherently suspect the media. As Karl said, "This is a newspaper that ridicules us, hates us, demeans us, thinks we are stupid and uneducated and backward, and it adds to my skepticism."

Charlie, a Moore supporter, suggests that Democrats consider their motives: "Imagine that Al Franken were running against Ted Cruz. Would you vote for Franken and why? Then, if Franken were further accused of misconduct with teenage girls, how would your vote change?"

As the Alabama GOP put it, "There is a sharp policy contrast between Judge Moore, a conservative Republican who supports President Trump, and the liberal Democrat who will fight and thwart the agenda of our president. We trust the Alabama voters in this election to have our beloved state and nation's best interest at heart. Alabamians will be the ultimate jury in this election—not the media or those from afar."

Voters in the Heart of Dixie are keenly aware that the spotlight is on them. Unless new information comes out in the next week, Roy Moore will be popping the champagne corks next Tuesday.

Taking on Iran's Nuclear Threat

I n the spring of 2015, six countries joined the United States in creating the Joint Comprehensive Plan of Action with Iran, a framework which ultimately led to the Iran Nuclear Deal. In essence, Iran agreed to significantly reduce its capacity to enrich uranium in return for the lifting of crippling economic sanctions. In May of 2018, Trump withdrew from the deal.

Treaties are usually technocratic exercises in diplomacy, and by their nature imperfect for all sides. Not this time. Trump, who said he knows deals, saw this as a bad one. And the reactions from voters were predictably split along political lines. If you backed Obama, you probably feel he got the best deal possible, stood firm with our allies, and hemmed in Iran to keep America safe. If you backed Trump, you probably felt his decision to exit the deal was far better, since the threat of America's military and financial might is a far better deterrent than a piece of paper signed by an untrustworthy theocracy.

Treaties—especially military alliances and deterrence deals—were once bipartisan exercises. Nearly all American politicians supported NATO. Nearly all were skeptical of Russia. In a more divided country, "bipartisan" is a thing of the past, and emotions tend to be more important than the actual content of a treaty. In the case of Iran, each side gathered its own facts to support its own viewpoint. Yet, in this particular case, fewer than 10 percent of my voters said that they read any details of the deal at all; as with other foreign policy issues, they read the headlines and stood with their leaders.

Voters on Iran: A Split Decision

May 18, 2018[11]

This past week, I asked 450 voters to rate—on a scale of 1 (for dissatisfied) to 10 (approval)—President Trump's decision to pull out of the Iran agreement. Although there is common ground in America on issues like gun control, DACA, and infrastructure, voters are very divided on America's exit from this deal, otherwise known as the Joint Comprehensive Plan of Action, or JCPOA.

"I'd give it a 1," writes Brenda from New Mexico. "This is one more spiteful move, contrary to the advice of our allies and our seasoned diplomats. Its purpose seems mainly to undo anything Obama accomplished—and it further discredits the US in the eyes of the world."

"Ten!" says Edward from Maryland. "The Iran deal was built upon a set of lies from Iran and the false premises promulgated by Obama and Kerry. At best, the deal delayed Iran's ability to acquire nuclear weapons while they screamed, 'Death to our neighbors and to America.'"

"Horrible!" writes Danielle from New York. "I have spent a lot of time in multiple college classes learning about US-Iran relations, and specifically this deal. It is foolish to think that Iran will cave to sanctions, and while the deal was not perfect, this betrays trust internationally and undermines our commitment to creating a more peaceful world."

"My take is that it's a 10," says Geoff from New Hampshire. "It was a one-sided deal to begin with, and a new agreement will strengthen our position. And, once again, it shows that when Trump says he'll do something, he delivers. Strength talks, while B.S. walks!"

It's a stunning example of polarization in the views of Americans.

Many voters dug into the details of the Iran issue, quoting everything from Fox News to John Oliver. Carol from Ohio went to the JCPOA website and reread the entire agreement before she sent in what she called "a big fat 10."

In the minds of voters across the country, there are three factors affecting their views:

1. Whether we got enough in return for lifting hundreds
    of billions of dollars in sanctions. To Trump supporters,
    we were focused too narrowly on nuclear capabilities,
    with no regard to ballistic missiles or the use of the
    money, which, they have read, is funneled to terrorist
    activities in Syria and Yemen. And, "The deal took
    all future nonmilitary options off the table." To
    nonsupporters of Trump's action, it was an imperfect
    deal, supported by our allies, that was working
    successfully as a deterrent.

2. Whether this deal hurts us or helps us with North
    Korea. Those who disapprove of Trump's decision
    believe that our exit demonstrates that you cannot
    rely on the United States to keep its promises. On the
    other hand, those who agree with the decision believe
    this move demonstrates that "the US will no longer

be manipulated into spineless, ridiculous deals with terrorist dictators who hate us."

3. Whether they trust that Trump made this decision with extensive thought, input, and conversation with allies. The anti-Trumpers believe that this was a rash campaign promise, made by an uninformed president who will reject anything done by Obama. The supporters of the agreement see the president meeting with international allies, consulting with his team, and accessing much more intelligence than we have.

If there is any common ground at all in the minds of voters, it's the ephemeral nature of executive power. Any deal done without the approval of Congress just might be a deal without teeth, and voters are wondering whether Trump will strike a North Korean agreement on his own without ultimately reaching out to lawmakers for their blessing.

And few are surprised about the decision. After all, this is a president who does what he says he's going to do—even when those promises are alarming.

The Brett Kavanaugh Nomination Becomes a Partisan Circus

In the fall of 2018, Donald Trump got his second of three chances to nominate a Supreme Court justice and change the ideological makeup of the court. He nominated the judicial conservative Brett Kavanaugh.

The Kavanaugh hearings went about as you might expect, devolving into a partisan battle about Kavanaugh's credentials and judicial positions. But that all changed when, after the hearings had already closed, accusations of sexual misconduct surfaced. Christine Blasey Ford, a psychology professor, had sent a letter to a senator accusing Kavanaugh of assaulting her when both were in high school. In the end, the FBI investigated, Ford testified, Kavanaugh denied the allegations, and we all got treated to a sordid romp through the antics of a bunch of drunken high-schoolers in the 1980s. Kavanaugh was confirmed with a two-vote margin; not a single Republican voted against him.

Brett Kavanaugh's nomination to the Supreme Court featured everything we've come to expect from partisan infighting: last-minute accusations of sexual impropriety, hearings conducted for shock value, and a vote along party lines in which no scandal—certainly not one from decades ago—can stop party ideologues from pushing their preferred candidate across the finish line.

It also captured the attention of the electorate. The emotion that I heard from voters in reaction to these hearings lasted long after Kavanaugh was confirmed. Even in 2020, there were people who told me that these hearings were a major factor in why they voted for a particular presidential candidate.

Kavanaugh Nomination Has Turned into a Circus

September 25, 2018 [12]

What do you think of when you hear the word "circus"? The trapeze artist, the lion tamer, the clowns, the acrobats—all under the big top, in a frenzy of activity? If you ask voters what they think of Congress's handling of the nomination of Brett Kavanaugh to the Supreme Court, the most common word they use is "circus," connoting a group of senators, in the center of a tiered arena, all trying to grab our attention without accomplishing much.

"The hearings were a circus," said Dan, a Republican from Minnesota. "The Republicans were on one side, praising the judge, while the Democrats were in another ring, adding plenty of drama."

"It was a bad episode of *House of Cards*," offered Chuck, an independent from Oregon, "with key leaders all trying to make each other miserable. As a viewer, I didn't like any of the acts."

It's been a little over two weeks since the four days of confirmation hearings before the Senate Judiciary Committee. Nominated in July by Trump, and lauded by the president as a man with "impeccable credentials,"[13] Kavanaugh endured a process that became what Justice Ruth Bader Ginsburg called "a highly partisan show"—and that was before the sexual assault allegations by Professor Christine Blasey Ford came out in public, and before the newest allegations from Deborah Ramirez.

The 500 voters I speak with weekly wrote me unsolicited notes, asking whether I was going to explore "the circus" with them—and I took the bait. Surely, regular American citizens would find some common ground, some reasonable way through all of the drama we have been experiencing.

No such luck.

Although most Americans agree that there is a frenzy, Republican and Democratic voters are divided about who is to blame for the drama. Most voters, however, are not talking about Kavanaugh and his credentials—or even the accusers. Instead, they are lambasting the other party.

Most Democrats see the process as one big Republican strategy to "Get the Conservative Judge Through As Fast As Possible." They are angry at Senators Chuck Grassley, Orrin Hatch, and Mitch McConnell, whom they believe are pushing, prodding, rushing, and ignoring the seriousness of the allegations. Said Julian from Massachusetts, "I am pissed that [Merrick] Garland was held up for almost 300 days and we're at day 70 and Republicans are trying to ram Kavanaugh through despite serious dishonesty and obvious lying on his part." Or, said Ruth from New Jersey: "It's really hard for me to watch these white guys setting deadlines, blatantly pushing Kavanaugh through, and doing the same disgusting thing with Christine Ford that they did with Anita Hill: belittling and insulting her—all in the name of getting their hyper-conservative candidate in."

Across the board, Democrats see this as a set of manipulative tactics on the part of Republicans to force their guy through and ignore the legitimate claims of a sexual assault survivor who finally has the courage to speak out. Voters are appalled that the response of Republicans to the accusations sends a message to teenage sons that their actions in high school or as a college freshman have no bearing on their futures. As Jeremy from New Hampshire said, "The most important thing to me is that there's an investigative and deliberative process that's fair to everyone involved. The fact that we have a hastily scheduled showdown is disgusting to me."

Republican voters generally tell a different story: that the process is a desperate and political attempt by the Democrats—a last resort—to disqualify Kavanaugh at any cost. Here's how Peter from Illinois sees it: "The Dems played a crap hand into a real winner. They didn't have the votes, but they had an ace in the sleeve. They knew of the letter and leaked it to the press, which forced Dr. Ford to go public when it was too late for Trump to pull Kavanaugh and submit a replacement before the midterms. Well played." Or, said Joseph from Texas: "It's just so damned predictable that this was going to happen. We all knew that there would be some story at the eleventh hour about how Kavanaugh was either racist or sexist."

At the core of the Republican point of view is disbelief that Senator Dianne Feinstein held onto a letter for three months and didn't show it to anyone. Her excuse about the privacy of the victim doesn't seem credible to them. As Hugh from California said, "Feinstein's stunt is a new low, that will surely blow up in the faces of the Democrats." And now, Republican voters are focused on how Ramirez came forward only after six days of consulting with a Democratic lawyer, and most people expect that there will be more allegations this week.

There was only one area of agreement: over 85 percent of my voters believe that Ford and other accusers should be heard prior to any final vote. Said Nancy, a Republican from Connecticut, "If the Republicans do not give this air, in spite of the circus it will likely cause, I think they deserve to be voted out of office."

Although we don't know what the outcome of this frenzy will be, it's clear that the big loss is for the American people, who have become cynical about their leaders. And that's the common ground: voters from both parties believe that Congress is incapable of running a process, unable to work together, and full of politicians who are mostly concerned with grandstanding for their next elections—focused on themselves.

No matter what happens here, no one will win. If Democrats block Kavanaugh's nomination, they'll likely have to go through it all again with another conservative nominee. If Republicans vote Kavanaugh through after the hearings, they'll have to deny the legitimacy of reports of sexual assault. Either way, the Supreme Court will lose its last remaining shreds of nonpartisan decency and credibility. Our government has been replaced by a circus, and the voters are not entertained.

Trump Takes On "The Squad"

I n the 2018 midterm election, four liberal women were elected to Congress for the first time. Two were democratic socialists: Alexandria Ocasio-Cortez, a Latina, and Rashida Tlaib, a Muslim of Palestinian descent. The other two were Ilhan Omar, a Somali refugee who is Muslim, and Ayanna Presley, a Black woman who had upset a ten-term congressman in the Democratic primary. Together, they became known as "The Squad." As a Bostonian, I know Ayanna Pressley, who is one of the most talented policymakers and advocates I have ever met.

Because of their views and their backgrounds, The Squad was an irresistible target for Trump, who, in a three-tweet thread,[14] said, "So interesting to see 'Progressive' Democrat Congresswomen, who originally came from countries whose governments are a complete and total catastrophe, the worst, most corrupt and inept anywhere in the world (if they even have a functioning government at all), now loudly and viciously telling the people of the United States, the greatest and most powerful Nation on earth, how our government is to be run ... Why don't they go back and help fix the totally broken and crime infested places from which they came. Then come back and show us how it is done. These places need your help badly, you can't leave fast enough." When challenged on his comments, he doubled down, adding, "We will never be a Socialist or Communist Country. IF YOU ARE NOT HAPPY HERE, YOU CAN LEAVE! It is your choice, and your choice alone. This is about love for America. Certain people HATE our Country."

Telling someone to "go back where they came from" is a barely veiled racist trope, especially since three of the congresswomen were born in America. The majority of Democratic and independent voters saw the tactic for what it was: a vicious attempt by the president to feed red meat to his base. In fact, in a press conference the following day, Ayanna Pressley called the tweets a "disruptive distraction" and advised Americans, "Do not take the bait."

When voters reacted to Trump's tweets, I decided that instead of just synthesizing their comments into themes, I would share their verbatim comments in my column.

Trump vs. The Squad—Voters Weigh In
July 18, 2019 [15]

Over the last several days, I have been in conversation with my panel of 500 voters about the conflict between President Trump and four progressive Democratic congresswomen. The general themes I have heard are:

- Shock that Democrats are taking the bait, one more time, as if it is news that the president made a racist remark.

- Disgust that our president has stooped this low.

- A belief that this is a smart and devious ploy by Trump to position the four women as the heart and soul and face of the Democratic Party, labeling them—and all Democrats—as radical socialist America-haters.

For a deeper dive, here is a sampling of notes written to me by some of the voters on my panel:

Joseph, a Republican from Texas:

Wow, what an explosive message from Trump! My initial reaction was shock. Was this political suicide? I read it again and admitted that these are my thoughts too.

I know I'm not a racist. I am Hispanic, and I didn't feel it was a racist tweet. I don't think anyone knows what racism is anymore. It's used so often, it's lost its bite. Not a single person in his base left because of that tweet, and I think it actually did more to raise awareness about what these particular Democrats have been spewing for a while, which is much more racist if you consider the anti-Semitic quotes from one of them.

They won't denounce Antifa, not even for the assault on an ICE center where the American flag was replaced with the Mexican flag.[16] My president says what he feels like no other politician has ever done, and lives with the consequences. It may cost him an election, but he never strikes out while letting the pitch sail by. I'll take that over running and hiding. We've got a country to run. We need people who love our country and want to make it the best possible place to live. I guess that's why they come here in droves.

Nina, a Democrat from Michigan:

He is a racist. Anyone still supporting him is a racist. I am furious and upset Every. Single. Day. I can barely think straight. I keep upping my game of wearing politically "provocative" clothing. I find myself sizing people up in public, watching and waiting for people to be offensive. I don't know what my reaction will be, but I am enraged.

He is disgusting. I want him impeached, yesterday.

Julian, a Democrat from Massachusetts:

I find the whole thing infuriating and sadly all too familiar as a half-Asian, half-European, first-generation American. Under even the weakest microscope, the sentiment is stupid. What makes you more American than me? Your skin color? You are conveniently forgetting everyone that got here before you or your ancestors; and even then, it's a stupid argument. American-ness is not about who got here first, because we all know who that was. American-ness is about the values you hold. And those values are pretty damn well stated in the Declaration of Independence and the Constitution. Your rights are the same as mine. Doesn't matter what you believe or worship. Doesn't matter what you look like. That's what the flag stands for.

Tim, an independent who voted for Trump, from Colorado:

What an idiot. He can't seem to stay out of his own way. The only thing I can think of is that he feels the more that AOC and the others are in the spotlight, the more it makes Democrats look really liberal, which will put off the moderate voter. But it equally makes me dislike Trump, so it leaves me feeling left without a choice in 2020.

Katie, a Republican from North Carolina:

I don't care much for any of those women, but as usual, Trump needs to be more mindful of what he says. Show a little maturity and restraint. But I guess that's why a lot of people like him.

Suzy, a Republican from Ohio:

All five of them need to stand in a corner. No doubt that Trump is oafish. As soon as I heard it, I rolled my eyes. OMG... could he have started a bigger fire?

My hopes are that soon someone lets him know that when his opposition is slinging mud at each other, he might wanna sit back and watch and not step in the fray.

Kathryn, a Democrat from Massachusetts:

I'm really ashamed of top-ranking Republicans. Regardless of how you feel about the politics of this particular group of women, telling brown people to go home is classic. Finally, do we really need to see who votes on whether Trump said a bad thing? Do we really need to vote on a resolution to call this guy America's Racist Uncle in Chief at this point?

Nancy, an independent who voted for Clinton, from Connecticut:

I have begun to be shell-shocked by this president. My first reaction was horror of the words posted and Republican leadership's reactions (or lack thereof), and my second reaction was that we should not make so much of his stupid tweet bombs and maybe he wouldn't continue to behave as such a juvenile in public.

David, a Republican from Pennsylvania:

The Democrats have no trouble singling out Trump for a supposedly racist statement, but they could not do the same thing to Representative Ilhan Omar a few weeks ago. It had to be "softened" to a general statement condemning all hateful statements. Give me a break. The hypocrisy is breathtaking! (But not surprising.) A pox on both their houses. I don't think Trump is racist, but he is stupid. The Squad accused Pelosi of being racist a few days ago. They all suck. This will most likely lead to four more years of Trump. Republicans are stuck with Trump. Democrats are just stuck—we could use a good candidate!

Jeremy, a Democrat from Massachusetts:

If you remove the racial dimension, Trump's attacks on the four lawmakers are deeply problematic for other reasons. I disagree with far-left politicians like AOC about many things. But I also recognize that dissent and critique play important roles in maintaining the health of our society—and also in pushing us collectively toward the types of introspection that make a better future possible. To me it seems the discourse in Trump's tweet is intended to delegitimize dissent in ways that are deeply corrosive to the long-term health of democracy.

Jim, a Republican from Pennsylvania:

This is the USA—and both sides have freedom of speech.

If burning the flag can be considered a legal form of protest, why can't sending a tweet saying, "If you don't like it, get out"?

No one has ever seen anything like Trump—and that is fantastic in many ways. Why? More people are getting actively involved in politics than I can remember in my lifetime, whether they love him or not.

A lot of people like Trump, as arrogant and narcissistic as he may come across at times, because, quite frankly, he focuses on the issues that need to be fixed.

The house is having an emergency vote on his "tweets"? Why don't they focus on their job and fix problems like immigration at the border?

Pat, a Democrat from Washington:

I'll admit my first impression of the four new congresswomen is that I wasn't a fan of them. They seemed more adept at getting media attention than actually doing the job.

I always tell myself I'm not going to be surprised because Trump has revealed over and over this is who he is, but here I am surprised. As for Congresswoman Omar, who actually did immigrate here, I can't think of a more hurtful and poisonous thing to say to an immigrant. The reaction by the GOP to Omar as a whole reminds me of when Obama first took office; it's a loathing so extreme that the bigotry behind it is obvious.

Dan, an independent from Minnesota:

I was really disappointed in Trump's comments, because I came to the realization that it's entirely possible that he is personally not racist, but he has no problems exploiting race as an issue to divide people for his own benefit. He is, after all, a businessman, and I can see him justifying this kind of rhetoric as "just business" in his own mind. I think that's just as bad, if not worse than racism itself. Also, I worry about how the relative silence from the GOP will normalize this kind of rhetoric.

Robert, a Republican from Massachusetts:

I have a hard time believing the president is this brilliant. Maybe some of his campaign people came up with the strategy to start a debate with the four congresswomen. By starting this political storm with The Squad and getting every Democrat riled up, it could be putting a new face on the party that he will be running against in 2020. This strategy could draw back many independents and moderates who got him elected the first time.

Biden Hunkers Down during the Pandemic

I n the spring of 2020, the coronavirus was spreading widely, states were locking down, and Donald Trump was flailing. Meanwhile, Joe Biden, the presumptive nominee of the Democrats was… pretty much invisible.

The voters on my panel universally thought this seemed like a poor choice for a prospective leader. They believed that Biden needed to introduce himself and get out in front of withering criticism from President Trump. Having experienced a president who was so highly visible—through rallies, public appearances, and thousands of tweets—they wondered who this new guy running for the position was. How did he expect to become president without connecting with voters? Biden's challenge was exacerbated by the pandemic, which kept him from participating in events and restricted him to making statements from his basement in Delaware.

As weak as this position appeared at the time, it may have been effective. Biden stayed home, stayed safe, planned and plotted. Trump shouted, tweeted, railed, and failed to make significant progress in the fight to keep the country safe from a rapidly spreading infectious disease.

In the end, though, hunkering down gave many voters the feeling that Biden was just too tired to inspire them, and too weak to empathize with their situations. Debunking that impression will be critical if President Biden wants Americans to see him as a strong and capable leader.

The Nation Is in Crisis. Where Are You, Joe Biden?

April 22, 2020 [17]

As President Trump speaks daily to Americans about the coronavirus, his presumed opponent, former vice president Joe Biden, is invisible. At least that is what more than 80 percent of the voters on my panel of 500 tell me. It's not just Trump supporters; more than half of Democrats feel this way also.

"He's been silent on the national and world stage," said Joseph, a Democrat from Massachusetts. "His social media presence is pathetic, and that is especially tragic, since it's going to be a centerpiece of communication as we work our way out of this situation."

His outreach to millennials has been ineffective, according to young voters on my panel who backed Senators Bernie Sanders and Elizabeth Warren. Steven, a Democrat from New York, said that the message "Vote for me to get rid of Trump" doesn't resonate with him or his friends; nor does a plea from their parents' generation just to swallow the pill. "We want to know what Biden will accomplish for us beyond the election, and how he's going to do it." Added Charles from Massachusetts, "As a person of color, I just feel that Biden needs to earn my vote and reach out to me on the issues I care about."

It's not like Biden isn't trying. He announced a new plan for unemployment insurance, has conducted virtual town halls, and has appeared on television. But most people on my panel haven't noticed—and are wondering when Biden will demonstrate that he can still lead.

Despite Trump's low approval ratings, this is a problem for Democrats: in light of uncertainty about the coronavirus this November, it's clear that the presidential election will be all about turnout. Americans who are charged up about their candidate—like Suzy from Ohio, who said that she will get to the polls even if she is on her deathbed—are the ones candidates can rely on. Yet, according to a recent survey[18] by ABC and the *Washington Post*, Trump is winning the enthusiasm race. Whereas 53 percent of Trump supporters are very enthusiastic, only 24 percent of Biden supporters are. Building these numbers up is Job One for the Biden campaign.

What should Biden do? Lay low and pounce later, or move now? Voters are split on strategy.

The Do Nothing camp believes that it's fine for Biden to stay quiet for now and let the president implode. "Limited exposure is not such a bad idea, and he should stay away from too many rambling interviews," said Robert, a Democrat from Massachusetts. "He can't compete with Trump for airtime, and so he should not panic about it."

These voters believe that the Biden team should prepare for what they believe will be a vicious onslaught in the fall, featuring constant messages suggesting that Biden suffers from dementia. Additional attacks on Hunter Biden's business dealings in Ukraine could cast doubt on Joe Biden's promise to bring integrity back to the White House. Smart action in these areas will be critical, said Lynda, a Democrat from Minnesota, "and they need to be as wicked as the Trump team will be."

The Do Something camp takes a different view, recommending several strategies for Biden and his campaign team.

One is to grab headlines by announcing his vice-presidential pick, along with a wish list of cabinet members. Key to this would be a strong Treasury secretary who will be able to help manage a fragile economy, and a strong head of Health and Human Services, such as one of the governors who is visibly leading during the pandemic. Regarding the VP pick, no prospective candidate generated widespread enthusiasm other than Michelle Obama. Said Denise from Texas, "If I were Joe Biden, I would camp out on Michelle Obama's doorstep until she says yes."

Another popular strategy was to acknowledge that Biden has never been good speaking off the cuff, and to focus on speeches (with teleprompters) and advertising. Among many others, David, a Democrat from North Carolina, suggests a video campaign that promotes what he calls "Biden's biggest leadership assets: his empathy, trustworthiness, and honesty."

Even if waiting is what his strategists counsel, Biden probably should recognize that it will be hard to outfight Trump from a standing start. Amid shortfalls of testing supplies, with the federal government swooping in to confiscate medical supplies ordered by states, death tolls surging, and Trump tweeting in support of protests from recklessly impatient "patriots" in places like Michigan, the president's administration appears strident and disorganized in a national crisis. This is a time for leadership, as the nation's governors are demonstrating. The time for Biden to show he can lead is now—and for all the coming months until November. Leaders don't hide from a crisis. Neither should Biden.

Trump Loses the First 2020 Presidential Debate

O n September 30, 2020, Joe Biden and Donald Trump held the first presidential debate of the 2020 general election.

Except that it wasn't really a debate. It was a shouting match, in which President Trump interrupted and harassed candidate Biden at every turn.

This did little to make anyone feel good. Biden was a 77-year-old man with a speech impediment—and looked like one. Trump is a loud bully—and looked like one. Voters were just embarrassed that this is how their candidates behaved. And the language that they used to describe that evening didn't exactly make us proud of our great democracy.

Biden entered the night ahead eight points in the polls.[19] A week later he was ahead by nine points. That was hardly a surge of epic proportions.

Looking back on this night, it seemed to represent how we act as voters and as a nation. We shout at and berate each other. And after it's done, nobody gets convinced and nobody feels good.

It's probably too much to ask for candidates to listen to each other in the future. But as citizens, we could certainly do better at listening to people who disagree with us.

Voters Weigh In on the Debate: Trump Lost the Night

October 1, 2020 [20]

"I looked for the debate on television last night, but I couldn't find it," said Tom, a Democrat from North Carolina. "Instead, I watched a program where an older gentleman was trying to have a conversation with an immature child having a temper tantrum."

Most of the 150 voters on my 500-person panel who weighed in on the first presidential debate Tuesday night, independent of party, agreed, using the word "embarrassing" to best describe the debacle we watched last night. The chart below lays out the responses; the larger the word, the more frequently it was mentioned.

About 70 percent of Democratic presidential nominee Joe Biden's supporters felt their candidate had won, particularly because he stayed calm in the midst of the chaos. "I thought he did pretty well, considering how absolutely intolerable it is to have someone tell lies about you whenever they open their mouth," said Kathryn, a Democrat from Massachusetts. Thirty percent of Democrats thought it was impossible to pick a debate winner. Democrats did report that Biden seemed flat, missing opportunities to look into the camera and remind Americans that they were watching their leader.

Independents were not impressed, with many reporting they turned their televisions off after watching two angry candidates flinging barbs at each other. "I guess if I were a school kid, I would say that 'Trump started it!' because Trump went on the attack and never stopped," said Joel, an independent from upstate New York. Joel doesn't plan to watch any more debates, but he says he will probably vote for Biden.

Although some voters in President Trump's base believed that their candidate was strong and dominating—in a good way— about half were unhappy with the president's performance. Lynn, a Republican from Pennsylvania, called him "agitated" and "too hostile," while Katie, a Republican from South Carolina, said, "The entire evening consisted of name-calling and interrupting— especially by Trump. He was rude and immature." Lynn and Katie haven't changed the way they will vote, but they're hopeful the next debate will be better and more informative.

Many voters believed Biden's best line was about Trump's performance: "Under this president, we have become weaker, sicker, poorer, more divided, and more violent." As Dan, an independent from Michigan, noted, "Biden probably should have just repeated that line all night long, interspersed with reminders about the two key metrics we should keep in mind: $750 and 200,000."

The Controversy over Voter Fraud

Written for this book in February 2021.

In the 2020 presidential election, Vice President Joe Biden received 81 million votes to President Donald Trump's 74 million votes and Biden won the Electoral College 306–232. Looking at these numbers, it's difficult to call Biden's win anything other than a clear victory. But Donald Trump predicted fraud months before the election, blaming massive numbers of unverified mail-in ballots, a raft of votes from dead Americans, corrupted voting technology, and so on. This "Big Lie" got significant traction over 2020, motivating tens of millions of voters to believe that the election was indeed rigged.

Nan, a Democrat from Connecticut, is confident in the election results. "When I see that dozens of lawsuits across the country were filed, considered, and rejected by the courts—especially with Republican-appointed judges—that's enough for me," she said. "And even more, when the chief cybersecurity officer of the United States says that ours was the most secure election ever, we need to move on." (Nancy was referring to a statement by Christopher Krebs,[21] the director of the Cybersecurity and Infrastructure Security Agency, who was fired by Trump two weeks after the November election.) Most Democrats echo Nan's thoughts. Said Andy, a Democrat from Minnesota, "The election was not rigged, which I can say with confidence considering the courts, intelligence agents, and local election officials who validated this. This reveals the hypocrisy of people who often refer to progressives as 'snowflakes,' yet throw a tantrum when their candidate loses, and it is disheartening."

The primary evidence my Democratic voters relied on was that 61 of 62 lawsuits filed by attorneys for Trump were thrown out by judges, including federal judges appointed by the president.[22]

But Andy and Nan don't listen to the same officials as Beth does. She is a Republican from Michigan who says she "seriously believes the election was stolen." Most of her evidence comes from watching local controversy about the returns in her state. One was a claim, all over her news, that Republican poll watchers were being banned from entering the TCF Center in Detroit. (In fact, there were already more than 134 poll watchers inside the arena, which was the maximum allowed.[23]) Beth also heard several stories about absentee ballots arriving in passenger vans and military ballots being transferred by hand onto machine-readable ballots—all of which were actually standard procedure, but which Republicans portrayed as sinister and illegal. She said, "There are just too many fishy situations. And besides, I have a friend who received a ballot for her mother, who is now deceased—which is proof that the system is a mess."

Among the Republican voters on my panel, about half believe that Biden won the election legitimately, and the other half believe there was enough election fraud that the winner was probably Donald Trump. That would mean that there are more than 35 million Americans who are like Beth. As I explored this, it became clear that the dominant factor in why people claimed fraud was related to mail-in ballots. Specific concerns from voters were that, as Alan, a Republican from New York, said, "There were all of these ballots mailed to citizens and returned without any proof the submitter is who they claim to be. When I was in the military, my ballot had to be executed in person at the base and certified by military officials. This time, the potential for fraud is obvious." Others echoed Alan's sentiments and were especially concerned about the states in which ballots did not require a request initiated from the voter.

Of course, the other cause of these opinions about fraud was the president himself, who, according to Politico, tweeted about voter fraud 127 times between March and October of 2020.[24] A Gallup poll reported an 11-point drop in voter confidence in elections from 2018 to 2020 (from 70 percent to 59 percent) and a 34-point drop in confidence among Republicans[25]—an alarming metric that demonstrates that Trump's message got through.

Even among the Democrats in my panel, there is waning confidence in the system. Over half of them believe that there were irregularities in the process—just not enough to change the election results. And when I asked voters what would increase their confidence, most supported an investigation. "I believe that Biden won the election, but I think that dismissing fraud claims just because of a bunch of dismissed lawsuits is insufficient," said Barry, a Republican from Iowa. "I mean, the Democrats think there is Russian collusion, and we get a massive investigation by the government. We need that to ensure that this never happens again."

Barry has a point. It's clear that voters who have lost confidence in the election don't buy the evidence they have seen thus far. They want to be heard rather than being told that their views are crazy. Voters from both parties would welcome a bipartisan commission on elections that would focus on what the United States needs to do to restore confidence, fix broken processes, and make it easier for people to vote legitimately. If run well, such a commission would also determine the truth of, and likely reject, the myth that illegitimate Democratic votes, especially from people of color, were responsible for Trump's loss, a critical action to take as we look to 2022.

We won't get very far with pulling the country together when some red-state Republicans are passing laws that make it more difficult for minorities to vote, and some blue-state Democrats are sending ballots by mail to every voter. We can't have two separate voting systems in America, or systems that shift every time the governorship and the legislature change parties in a state. A bipartisan compromise that makes it easier to register to vote—and easier to get a mail-in ballot while ensuring the identity of citizens casting votes—would go a long way toward making systems transparent, convenient, and dependable. We can order groceries, choose who to date, and get prescriptions delivered with an app. Surely we can figure out a better way to vote that would make voters of all parties more confident in the system.

The Siege on Capitol Hill

Written for this book in February 2021.

"I t's not really complicated for me to understand why my three friends went to Washington, DC, to protest on January 6," said Katherine, a Republican from South Carolina. "Where I come from, if the president says the election was rigged and stolen by the Democrats, and if I hear reporters say that it's true, and if I see videos of people talking about fraud, and if my congressman agrees with it all, I believe it's my civic duty to protect our democracy."

Katherine told me that her friends did not go into the Capitol that day, but that they marched and protested peacefully along with thousands of others. "I know you are going to tell me I am racist, but I just can't understand the difference between what my friends did and the Black Lives Matter protesters after the death of George Floyd. In both cases, there were lots of peaceful protesters, but what we saw on TV was rioting, burning, looting, and destruction."

Most of the voters in my panel of 500 are upset about the storming of the US Capitol on January 6, and people from all points on the political spectrum have told me they were alarmed, disgusted, shocked, and saddened by what they saw, especially the physical destruction of property and the death threats hurled at elected officials. But there is still a difference in perspective. While Democrats see this as an outrageous and unprecedented violent act, some Republicans saw it as an escalation and continuation of the protests, riots, and violence that have been happening around the country for many months.

Although many commented on the sheer violence and destruction, others had more specific concerns. Some were shocked at the justifications. "The Capitol insurrection is a national embarrassment that will haunt me for the rest of my life," said Angus, a Democrat from Wisconsin. Angus was especially disturbed by the Christian rhetoric that was prominent at the riot. "Jesus said, 'Blessed are the meek,' not, 'Blessed are those who attempt to overthrow their government,' and an event like this should not be tied to the church."

Others, like Tim, an independent from Colorado, were troubled that "people were able to get into the Capitol where there was such a lack of preparedness and security." But there was some sympathy with the protesters' antigovernment feelings as well. Katie, a Massachusetts Democrat, confessed that although she was horrified by the destruction, she understood some of the actions by protesters. "To be completely honest, if I somehow found myself teleported into Mitch McConnell's office on the day of the event, I absolutely would have stolen his name tag off of his desk and smoked a cigar in his chair. Terrible, right?"

Most voters also told me they believed that those who stormed the Capitol were the fringe: the genuine anarchists, white supremacists, and would-be terrorists who can't be called Trump supporters, any more than Antifa rioters should be labeled "Democrats." Said Chrissie, a Republican from New Jersey, "When I saw Katie Couric lumping Trump supporters together with those animals at the Capitol—and saying that we needed to be deprogrammed—it made me so angry and frustrated. Who is she to be so condescending?"

Added Jane, a Republican from New Hampshire, "Forty Trump rallies before January 6 all around the country without a broken window or a blade of grass disturbed—and no one talks about that."

Where we seem to be most divided is in whether the actions on January 6 are an exceptional occurrence, or whether they reflect events and the increasing lack of tolerance on both sides of the political aisle.

When I asked about that, most Democrats said they saw the storming of the Capitol as a catastrophic and unique capstone to the Trump presidency, where the perpetrators need to pay the consequences and for which former President Trump bears the responsibility.

Trump supporters saw it as one more symbol of the anger in the United States, one more riot, one more response to violent rhetoric from leaders.

"People who are okay with protesters storming the federal buildings in Portland, Oregon, but not okay with DC, have just learned something about themselves," said Charles, an independent from Oregon. Others talked about the damage done by the 2017 Women's March on Washington, including more than 217 arrests, six injured police officers, and three vehicles set on fire, for which the media mostly reported a peaceful and passionate protest highlighting key issues such as reproductive freedom.

I asked these voters about President Trump's words, which seemed clearly to motivate people to walk down to the Capitol and show what he called "strength." Many in my sample of Republicans feel that Trump was echoing the rhetoric they have heard on the Democratic side over the last several years:

"He'd better have an army if he thinks he is gonna walk down the street in New York." (Governor Andrew Cuomo)[26]

"When you are in the arena, you got to be ready to take a punch—and therefore you have to be ready to throw a punch—for the children." (Speaker Nancy Pelosi)[27]

"I have thought an awful lot about blowing up the White House." (Madonna)[28]

"If the president goes ahead and fires Robert Mueller, we would have people take to the streets. I believe there would be widespread civil unrest." (Congressman Ted Lieu)[29]

"When they go low, we kick them." (former Attorney General Eric Holder)[30]

We can claim that comparing January 6 to other events is a false equivalency because of the location and level of the destruction, but the anger and violence in our country are not coming just from one political party or one individual. For America to move forward, we need to understand the difference between peaceful protests and violence—and acknowledge and reject extremists of all stripes. We can never tolerate another violent siege like what happened on Capitol Hill. But protesters—and their supporters—will need to visibly adopt rules that promote "peaceable assembly." Police enforcement should reflect that, rather than giving rightist protesters leeway that's not accorded to those on the left.

In the end, unless we talk ourselves down from the cycle of violence that led to January 6, America cannot hold together as a nation.

Part II

Common Ground on the Issues

I can't blame you if, after reading the previous section, you feel depressed. As a nation, we have become quite adept at making assumptions about each other. Every event becomes another reason to be divided.

But there is hope. The hope comes from how people actually feel about the issues. Once you toss aside all the partisan posturing and dig down into what matters to voters, an amazing truth emerges: we agree on a lot—or at least we are willing to compromise on a range of policies that can move us forward as a nation.

We agree that guns ought to be legal and licensed, and that deranged people and ex-convicts shouldn't have them.

We agree that there should be a legal immigration system that rewards skilled people but prevents entry by those who evade the system.

We agree, for the most part, that climate change is an existential threat, and the government has a responsibility to save us from disaster.

And across the board, we agree that the rage in our country has to end.

As you'll read in the pieces that follow, there is plenty of common ground on policy. This is a crucial point, because much of our divisiveness comes from our perceptions of what we think others believe.

If only our leaders would recognize this common ground—rather than be seduced into scoring points at each other's expense—we might actually make some progress on the issues that matter to America. If there is a path back to sanity in American politics, these are the signposts along that path.

Shared Views
on Gun Control

I n October of 2017, Stephen Paddock shot and killed 60 people from a hotel window in Las Vegas and wounded 411 more. This, along with the rash of school shootings that plagues our country, is the reason we need to talk about guns—because the lives of innocent people are at stake.

The media narrative is that red-state conservatives oppose all gun control, and blue-state liberals want to take everyone's guns away. The media narrative is inaccurate.

My research with voters—and the results of national surveys— show that there is plenty of support for rational limits on guns. Over 80 percent of my voters support measures like waiting periods, closing the loophole of instant sales at gun shows with no background check, limits on anything that effectively creates a machine-gun-type automatic weapon (like the bump stocks that Stephen Paddock used), and limits on the size of magazines.

An obstacle here is not the electorate but the National Rifle Association (NRA), which is adept at stirring up fear and anxiety any time politicians begin to discuss reasonable limits on firearms.

But the NRA is now bankrupt, with its leaders accused of misuse of funds and corruption.[1] President Biden has called on Congress to ban assault weapons and adopt other gun control measures.[2] If there were ever a time that America could pass commonsense gun control legislation, now is that time.

Finding Common Ground on Gun Control

October 27, 2017 [3]

Jim is a 77-year-old conservative from Arizona. A lifetime member of the NRA, he got his first gun—a .22-caliber rifle—at age seven, when his grandfather decided he was old enough to learn about safety. He has owned guns ever since, and regularly takes target practice at a gun club. When Jim thinks about the shooting in Las Vegas, he tells me he believes we must get a handle on mental health, and that 99.9 percent of gun owners are not crazies.

Then, he surprises me.

"All of this said, our gun laws need significant improvement," Jim starts. "How about removing bump stocks from existence? Or requiring background checks on all gun show buyers?" Jim continues with detailed recommendations about mandatory waiting periods for gun purchases, regulations for ammunition sales, and more.

In my ongoing research with voters, there is significant common ground on gun control. Over 80 percent are supportive of additional regulation. Across the political spectrum, voters agree with Jim on universal background checks, waiting periods, banning sales of guns to people convicted of a violent crime, and much more—and this is supported by a recent national poll by Quinnipiac University.[4]

Unlike other issues I discuss with voters, the differences in their views about guns are more about personal experience and less about political affiliation. Their perspective depends on whether they live in Gun Country. Gun Country is defined neither by whether their state is red or blue nor by whom they voted for in the presidential election. It's more about their own community.

Voters outside of Gun Country denounce America's gun culture. They are concerned about America's 300 million guns, the media glorification of violence, and the number of children who get shot every year. They question why anyone would ever need an assault weapon and are especially negative about Congress's resistance to any legislative changes. While they don't necessarily believe that gun control would prevent mass shootings, they think it is a critically important step. Most want to close gun show loopholes, but have not been to a gun show; they want to ban assault weapons, but make no distinction between semi-automatic and automatic weapons; and they strongly support mandatory waiting periods for gun purchases, but would never actually buy one.

Other voters outside of Gun Country just don't have a lot of energy for the issue. Carl, a Trump supporter from New York, says, "I am a Republican, but this is not something I have a lot of interest in, as guns are just not part of my lifestyle."

In Gun Country, it's different.

"You have to realize that I was raised here," explains Sharon from Indiana. "We are law-abiding good country folk who just want to enjoy life and take care of our families, and we are not looking for an opportunity to annihilate our neighbors."

People in Gun Country talk about the zen quality they get from shooting a gun, the gratification they get from their ability to place a piece of lead in a target precisely. Jacob, an Ohio farmer, likens it to the feeling of a great baseball hit or a really good golf shot. Adds Leslie from North Carolina, "It's not uncommon here to have a lengthy discussion about guns with a perfect stranger and to actually bond over our shared interest."

Says Linda, a Clinton voter from South Carolina, "When I lived in Massachusetts, I never had any desire to own guns, because there was a general lack of interest in them by the public. Since being in the South, I have learned to shoot guns. I have bought guns, shipped and transferred guns, and even given them as gifts. It is a different world, and I know many women who love to shoot as much as men do."

In Gun Country, they also talk about having guns for protection in places where police aren't close by. Having a gun is like buying a home security system or a fire extinguisher. So when they talk about gun control laws, the conversation is more specific and technical.

Joe from Oklahoma explains, "Every time I buy a weapon at a retail dealer, I wait while they do the check, and it is rarely more than a half-hour delay. Honestly, some of the characters I have seen at gun shows would give me pause. I am also fine with new rules that limit clip capacity to maybe ten rounds for all rifles and pistols larger than .22-caliber."

Bruce, a Trump voter in Gun Country, puts it another way. "There is no need for assault rifles by civilians, or anything that converts such weapons to automatics. A fully automatic firearm can fire repeatedly and quickly as long as you hold down the trigger, but a semiautomatic fires only once when you pull the trigger. The weapon we need to ban is automatic—and that includes any gizmos that convert guns to automatic."

Why doesn't all of this support lead to progress on gun control legislation—or at least to restoration of the ban on high-capacity magazines and assault rifles championed by Ronald Reagan? Because of what Gun Country voters hear from the NRA.

The NRA spent $50 million in the last election to make sure members knew that "Hillary wants to take away all of your guns." Wayne LaPierre, the head of the NRA, famously told his membership that if the Democrats gain control of the government, "you can kiss your guns goodbye." Voters in Gun Country talk about a barrage of phone calls, postcards, and flyers from the NRA, explaining that Democrats are scheming to prevent the average private citizen from owning guns at all. The message from the NRA gets reinforced by anti-gun politicians on the other side who throw around terms that Gun Country sees as incorrect or misleading, such as using violent crime statistics in Chicago and generalizing them to the rest of the country. The result? Voters feel that the NRA may be overzealous, but that ardent advocates of increased gun control are completely out of touch with the culture of civility and responsibility that is part of their community.

For the people of Gun Country, as long as the NRA and the anti-gun extremists own the conversation, nothing can change. Instead of shared interests, we get a meaningful divide that doesn't need to exist in the first place.

There is common ground on gun control. Americans in and out of Gun Country are disgusted and horrified by events such as Las Vegas and agree that gun control is both important and inadequate in the face of those who have suffered. It's time to listen to one another and make progress.

Agreeing That We Hate the Divisiveness

By the summer of Trump's second year in office, I was able to get a pretty good idea of how voters were thinking about priorities, and it became clear that we had a lot of common ground. The main theme that arose from conversations with my panel, however, was our disdain *for each other*. And that disdain was based on a narrative about "the other side" that was untrue. We believed in extreme stereotypes about each other.

And we still do.

The Problem Isn't How We Feel About Trump—It's How We Feel About Each Other

July 18, 2018[5]

Is there enough common ground to build a new kind of dialogue about America?

It doesn't seem so. After all, Fox News and CNN/MSNBC appear to be broadcasting from different planets, with different audiences, different perspectives, different languages, and completely different sets of "facts." President Trump is either the savior finally forcing America to confront the tough choices it needs to make, or a toddler recklessly smashing the nation to bits.

There is no bridging the divide between Republicans and Democrats, between urban and rural, between the coasts and the middle of the country.

Or is there? I set out to find out where Americans agree and disagree. Last week, I asked my panel of 500 voters to rate 30 statements about policy, about the future of the country, and about some of Trump's recent decisions. To assess the areas of agreement and divisions, I segmented voters into four categories: liberals, moderate Democrats, moderate Republicans, and "Trump's base."

Where We Agree

As you might expect, 85 percent of my voters agreed on a number of statements of shared concern:

I worry about the state of our education system.

The federal deficit is a huge problem.

The decision about whether to have an abortion is excruciating for a woman.

I worry about the crumbling infrastructure.

I believe in the American Dream.

It is not a good idea to deport a veteran, even if they originally came to the United States illegally.

With the right training, an unemployed coal miner could learn to work in tech.

But these more obvious shared viewpoints are not the only places where we agree. Despite varying perspectives on guns, 90 percent of us agree that "guns should not be in the hands of anyone who is on the terrorist watch list." Nearly everyone, including most of those in Trump's base, believes that "there must be a better way to create immigration law than to separate children from families." And even those who wear Make America Great Again caps largely believe that "we should not boycott Harley-Davidson just because the company moves its manufacturing plant to Europe."

Ninety percent of us agree that "it's time for House Minority Leader Nancy Pelosi to step aside." Few of us want to see Starbucks CEO Howard Schultz run for president. And nearly 75 percent of us are skeptical about anything good coming out of the president's tariffs.

So there's widespread agreement not just on the obvious problems, but on where some of the proposed solutions are going awry. In all, 13 of the 30 statements on which I polled voters generated agreement.

Where We Are Divided

Not surprisingly, the more liberal you are, the less likely you are to agree that the world is safer because of the president's meeting with Korean leader Kim Jong-un, or that the Supreme Court confirmation should happen before November.

Moderates were more likely to believe it's time for a third political party, and that Mitt Romney should try another presidential run.

But there is a more substantial difference on what Trump's behavior means in historical perspective.

For example, Trump supporters are less likely to believe that Russian interference in our elections is a big problem. The logic, as one voter expressed it: "The United States has done that in other countries for years."

Does Trump lie more than any other president? This was the area where people disagreed the most. Liberals and moderates are certain that this is true. But voters in the Trump base offer the lies of past presidents, such as "You can keep your doctor" (Barack Obama), "We will investigate IRS corruption" (Obama), or "I did not have sexual relations with that woman" (Bill Clinton). "They all lie," wrote Anne from Michigan, who recalled how Franklin Delano Roosevelt hid his paralysis from Americans.

The other major area of division was voter response to this statement: "I have personally felt the benefits of tax reform." Somehow, hardly any of the liberal voters had benefited, but virtually all of the Trump supporters had.

What's going on here?

What matters most is your focus and your point of view. Trump voters see a president who lies like other presidents but delivers on their paychecks. Liberals see an egregious liar and focus less on the amount of withholding in their paychecks. We may live in the same America with the same president, but we don't see it the same way.

Demonizing Presidents Is Nothing New. Demonizing Voters Is.

The truly pernicious problem is what we think of each other.

Jill, a Trump supporter from New Hampshire, laid out her thoughts on what liberals believe: that socialism is better than capitalism; that Trump supporters are racist and stupid; that the United States needs a new constitution; that the United States would be better if there were no borders and anyone could come here and even vote; that criminal illegal immigrants are good for our country; that even healthy people who don't want to work should get paid by the government; and that abortion is a casual and easy decision for women. Do liberals really believe these things? I've polled them, and most don't.

Susan, a Democrat from Wisconsin, laid out her thoughts on what the Trump base believes: that minorities are a threat to our way of life; that everyone should have as many assault weapons as they want; that we should close our borders; that the president's tweets are a good thing; that Vladimir Putin is a leader to be admired; that the president should win a Nobel Peace Prize based on his work with North Korea; that a woman should never be president; and that former EPA administrator Scott Pruitt is a hero. I've polled the Trump base, and most don't believe these things, either.

Cable TV, campaign ads, and the filter bubble of Facebook are showing us a false picture of America: one where the other side is full of evil people who believe and do awful things. We see the worst of the people we disagree with and project this negative image to all of them.

But if there's one thing my research has shown, it's that we agree on more than we think.

There is room to build here. There is room for candidates who can reach across the divide and connect with people who share concerns about the deficit, about immigration, about reasonable gun control, about investing in infrastructure, and about our country's educational system.

The politics of hate are not what we are as a country ... at least not yet. We need to find people we disagree with on some things, and listen to them as basic human beings and Americans. We need candidates who treat media as a way to get a message out rather than a punching bag, and who recognize they will need to work with those with whom they disagree. We need a government that once again works for most of us.

That's not impossible, because what we agree on most is how distressing our divide is.

Immigration: Finding a Compromise

Immigration—how we regulate it, and how we enforce those rules—remains a central issue for Americans. And with President Trump's rallies, his scorched-earth tweets, and his photo ops at the border wall, he also made it practically impossible to find compromise solutions.

The result is that immigration is now more valuable as an issue to hit the other side over the head with than as an actual solvable problem. My voters see through all this posturing, but even so, it influences them.

This is tragic. Over the last decade, Congress has given serious consideration to bipartisan immigration compromises. The voters I spoke with on all sides of the issue had coalesced around a common set of policies, much as they have with gun control. These policies include strict rules for legal immigration, stronger border security, and a path to citizenship for the children of illegal immigrants who've been contributing to society.

But these are not slogans. "Democrats are for totally open borders" is a slogan—false, but repeated enough to influence views.

And "Republicans are against any immigration" is a counterslogan, also false.

If we can move beyond slogans, there is a compromise plan to adopt. The question is whether enough of our representatives in Congress have the courage to pursue it.

Immigration—the Problem Congress Doesn't Want to Solve
December 10, 2018 [6]

Immigration is a hot, contentious, emotional issue. President Trump warns of caravans full of criminals who are riddled with diseases. We feel helpless, seeing children separated from their parents at the Mexican border. After several false starts, Congress has yet to figure out whether to pay for a wall. And, the "Dreamers" (immigrants who were brought to the United States as children) still sit in fear, waiting to learn of their status.

As a nation, we have come to realize that this is an important problem to solve. When I first began discussing immigration with voters, in December 2016, only Trump's base rated it as a critical issue. Two years later, Democrats are paying much more attention, and they now rate its importance at 8 on a 10-point scale.

The conundrum: although voters long for a comprehensive immigration policy, the dysfunction in Washington makes this goal virtually unattainable. Even more, the narrative about immigration—generated by politicians who benefit from demonizing the other side—has unnecessarily divided us.

When I ask Americans how they feel about the current state of affairs, the top three words they use are "sad," "angry," and "embarrassed"—and they characterize the other political party's position as extreme and bullheaded. Republicans imagine that most Democrats demand fully open borders as the ultimate symbol of a truly compassionate society. Democrats will tell you that Republicans want our borders completely closed—because Republicans reject the notion that immigration is fundamental to our culture, economy, and values.

As I have discovered in the past with a range of issues, most Americans don't have such extreme views, regardless of where they sit on the political spectrum.

"I am so sick of people saying that I am opposed to immigrants," Colette, a Republican from Massachusetts, told me. "That's an ignorant statement and unfair. America is great because of our melting pot. I just don't think people should be let in without the correct paperwork." Fernando from New Jersey added, "I am an immigrant who came to the US from Cuba with my parents, and I know how tricky this issue is. And I reluctantly voted for Trump because I feel that it is unfair for people to come into the country illegally when other families are playing it fair and waiting for their turn."

Ken, a New York Democrat, admitted, "I am worried when my fellow Democrats talk about abolishing ICE (Immigration and Customs Enforcement). It sounds like they want open borders. It was never the party's policy and it is way too extreme." Added Catherine from Texas, "It is a vicious Trump talking point to suggest Democrats want no restrictions on immigration—but we do have laws and they should be enforced with a modicum of respect and compassion for the people seeking the same American Dream that most of our ancestors sought."

Voters from all ends of the political spectrum talk about their own families' immigration stories, and most understand the value of bringing new citizens to our country who want to work hard and build a better life. The majority support legal immigration, stronger border security, and a path to citizenship for Dreamers who have a clean criminal record and a commitment to paying taxes and learning English.

Americans are divided about a border wall, but they are willing to compromise: most Democrats I talked to are willing to build a wall as part of a more comprehensive immigration plan that keeps Dreamers in the United States. And most Republicans I talked to agree with Joseph from Texas: "Security is part of our lives: I'd never just let anyone walk into my home without an invite, I'd never shower with the curtain open, I always lock my car, and we can't enter office buildings without identification. Walls are everywhere." He adds, "You don't like a wall? If anyone has a better idea to secure our border, I am listening."

My overall impression is that voters on both sides are ready for a deal. So, why not just go back to the Comprehensive Immigration Reform Act of 2011, or CIRA, created by the then-bipartisan group of legislators who called themselves the "Gang of Eight," or push harder for the Border Security and Immigration Reform bill of 2018? And why do we think that we are much more divided than we actually are?

Because, as hundreds of voters told me, Congress and the president are simply unwilling to compromise. The issue is more valuable to them as a talking point and an attack strategy than as a problem to solve. Said Phil, a Republican from Idaho, "Why take immigration off the table when it gives our political leaders great face time on TV?" Added Jeremy, a Democrat from Maine, "My theory is that it's immature, divisive, small, and petty political leaders who are just afraid to take a stand and lose their primaries."

Dozens of voters related stories of politicians whose dominant campaign strategies were to exaggerate the viewpoints of the other party—and so it's no wonder that we think our country is so divided.

"In my Arizona district, both candidates raised millions yelling about immigration policy," said Anne. "I mean, why would you want to fix the issue when there is so much political and financial benefit to keeping it unresolved?" Bernadette, an independent from Kentucky, told me that she and her friends planned to vote for Democrat Amy McGrath, a retired Marine Corps fighter pilot, for Congress, until McGrath's opponent, Representative Andy Barr, created an attack ad criticizing McGrath's "dangerous agenda, which would open our borders and enable drug cartels to flood our towns with heroin and fentanyl." Leveraging this misinformation, Barr was able to convince voters like Bernadette, and he won. And people from the Sixth District in Kentucky learned a narrative about the other party that was not true.

Voters are ready for compromise, but they feel that the politicians who represent them are too afraid to occupy the no-man's-land where actual solutions exist. And so far, they're right. Every step toward compromise seems to generate searing reprisals from cable news, inflames more extreme primary opponents, and burns those who reach across the aisle. It's December 2018, and the courage and candor of our leaders—especially on critical issues like immigration—is at an all-time low.

Climate Change
Is a Crisis—and Most
of Us Know It

The news about the climate is dire. Weather extremes abound, the ice caps are melting, and it looks increasingly challenging to keep the earth's temperature below the two-degree-Celsius increase that would spell disaster.

If only voters would get together on this issue, there might be hope. Well, as it turns out, there is.

The Green New Deal—a grab bag that starts with climate and continues with issues from social justice to free college—was several steps too far for many of my voters. But ironically, it raised the profile of climate change enough to generate agreement that the climate part, at least, was a serious problem. When I connected with voters about the climate crisis in 2019, nine out of ten Democrats and half of Republicans rated it an urgent priority and were ready to take action.

The main impediment before 2020 was, as on so many other issues, the climate-skeptic-in-chief, Donald Trump. But President Biden, who started his term by rejoining the Paris Climate Agreement and canceling the Keystone XL pipeline, seems likely to focus on climate as a priority.

It's not clear in what form the US might take steps away from its headlong embrace of fossil fuels. But politics is about turning short-term crises into long-policy shifts. Every disastrous hurricane, flood, wildfire season, and polar vortex sending shivers through the middle of the country raises the profile of the issue. If the concern from the voters in my panel is any indication, there's a political deal to be made here, in the interests of the next couple of generations of Americans.

Climate Change Will Be a Decisive Issue in 2020

June 26, 2019[7]

In November 2018, a federal government report, filed by 13 agencies, laid out the damaging effects of climate change, along with a dismal set of projections about the future. President Trump's response to the report? "I don't believe it."

The president has been a consistent skeptic about climate change, but last week I decided to check in with my panel of 500 voters across the country—to see how they were thinking about the issue and its importance.

"I believe climate change is a very big problem, and I do want to be kind to Mother Earth," said Christina from New Jersey. "We need to get away from fossil fuels and it needs to be attacked from all angles." Although Christina sounds like a card-carrying member of the Sierra Club, she is actually a lifelong Republican and enthusiastic supporter of President Trump. And she is not alone. Colleen, a Republican from Massachusetts, believes that climate change is "very scary." When I say I am surprised that she, as a huge fan of Trump, feels that way, she explains that in this political climate, regular voters in her party are "misunderstood and underestimated," and more educated than Democrats would expect.

In fact, over the last few months, among the 500 people in my nationwide pool of voters, climate change has gone from an issue that was a top priority for only a few to one that a large majority believe is urgent to address. Over 90 percent of Democrats in my group rate addressing climate change as a top priority, and half of Republicans tell me they feel the same way. Over half of Democrats rate it a higher priority than addressing opioid addiction or election hacking or student loan debt. Among Republicans, there is still skepticism about whether humans caused the challenge we are facing, but paradoxically, there is general agreement that humans can do something about it.

We just might be approaching a tipping point, the term popularized by author Malcolm Gladwell to signify a moment of critical mass, when an idea spreads like wildfire. Voters tell me that their increased passion comes from a number of sources: their perception that our weather is just plain weirder, the recent announcement by Michael Bloomberg that he will invest $500 million of his own fortune in combatting environmental threats,[8] and messages coming from their children about the importance of safeguarding their lives. "When a grandchild looks her grandparent in the face and expresses concern for her future, the grandparent is more likely to pay attention," says Andrew, a meteorologist from Wisconsin. "We are more convinced by family members than by a graph—although I do love the data!"

An additional influencing factor is the creation of the Green New Deal, which has gone viral just as much as anything else championed by US Representative Alexandria Ocasio-Cortez of New York. (The manifesto was cosponsored with Massachusetts

Senator Edward Markey.) Virtually all voters have heard of it, and they have an opinion about it.

In general, Republicans and moderate Democrats give it a thumbs-down. "Talk about everything but the kitchen sink," says Joseph, a Democrat from Iowa. "It starts out well, but after climate change, it adds in other things like guaranteed income, and free college and health care. And all of those crazy Democratic candidates support it? With what money—and who are they kidding?" Even Katie, a liberal Democrat from New Hampshire, says, "The Green New Deal makes action look impossible because it sets all-inclusive, unrealistic goals."

Although voters don't necessarily support the details of the Green New Deal, they believe it is important to take action. As Emily Reichert, CEO of Greentown Labs, the phenomenal clean tech incubator in Somerville, tells me, "We are finally having a national conversation about climate change, and whether you like it or not, you have to give credit to the Green New Deal."

The tide is turning. The "Climate Kids" are suing the government in Juliana v. the United States;[9] the Sunrise Movement is building an army of young people to elect leaders who will take action on environmental issues; Republicans in Congress, like Cory Gardner of Colorado, tell crowds that "renewable energy presents the ultimate future for this country"; Representative Matt Gaetz, Republican of Florida, has proposed a Green Real Deal, focused on aggressively investing in clean-energy innovation; and states like New York and California are setting aggressive goals that strive for 100 percent renewable energy. At Greentown Labs, 210 companies have been created—and clean tech has already generated more than 110,000 jobs in the Massachusetts economy.

Nathaniel Stinnett, founder of the Environmental Voter Project, is on a mission to capitalize on this trend. His organization, via data analytics, has identified 15 million Americans who are environmentalists but who simply don't vote. The goal: take citizens who are passionate about addressing climate change and turn them into consistent activists, especially at the ballot box.

We clearly have resistance at the top. Just this past week, the Trump administration was accused of suppressing new Agriculture Department findings about the effects of climate change[10]—all this while the president and his leadership team promote fossil fuel use and eliminate environmental protections.

What I hear from American voters is that it is time for action. They are increasingly impatient, and most of the voters I talk to believe that the Trump administration is wrong on this issue, influenced by the oil and gas industry and other climate-change deniers. People want urgent, concrete, high-impact solutions: a carbon tax, significant investment in renewable energy, or regulations that move us away from a single-use, throwaway society. And there is enough common ground on this issue to make it pivotal for the 2020 election.

Yearning to Stop the Madness

By the end of 2019, voters all along the political spectrum told me they were experiencing exhaustion. They told me they were watching the news less, unable to stomach the disunion in their country. If there was one issue that Americans universally agreed on then, and still do now, it's their distress about our divisiveness. And they blame everyone from politicians to comedians to their unreasonable neighbors.

Most voters are burned out: sick of the hate, the rage, and the feeling that they want to pick their friends based on whether they would wear a mask at the local supermarket. As I learned over and over in my research, Americans don't believe we will all suddenly agree with each other, embrace each other, and sing "Kumbaya"— but they long to turn down the temperature.

Our Continental Divide
December 4, 2019 [11]

Does this sound familiar: "Every morning, I wake up with a pit in my stomach over how divided our country is. Sure, it's not as bad as the Civil War, but is that supposed to make me feel better?" asked Anna from Nevada.

Anna's sentiment is typical of citizens across the United States, no matter their politics. Over the last three years, there are many issues that my panel of 500 voters has disagreed on, but they consistently and overwhelmingly agree with the statement, "I am worried about the divisiveness in our country."

What's interesting is how voters diagnose the problem. Some feel it's "the other guys."

"It all started with Obama for me," said Phil, a Republican from South Dakota. "Hey, I'm a cop, and when our president started making a mockery of the police, it made me angry at everyone who agreed with him. For that, people started calling me racist, which is the worst thing anybody could call me when I know I'm not. So, I give up."

Helen, a Democrat from Delaware, thinks President Trump is at fault. "Trump took the Tea Party to new heights," she said. "He used all of that divisive language even before he became president. When you badmouth another group every day, you eventually lose them."

> *Rep. Adam Schiff illegally made up a FAKE & terrible statement, pretended it to be mine as the most important part of my call to the Ukrainian President, and read it aloud to Congress and the American people. It bore NO relationship to what I said on the call. Arrest for Treason?*
>
> **—Donald J. Trump (@realDonaldTrump)**
> *September 30, 2019* [12]

The list of culprits they cite is long—from Karl Rove to Adam Schiff to *Saturday Night Live*. And, although some blame individuals and parties, many voters still believe the divide is about policy and the role of the federal government. Robert from Massachusetts agreed, "Republicans are concerned about socialistic policies: too much government, too many intrusive laws and regulations, overly pro-labor, too much attention being paid to income inequality—and now it's out of hand."

Of course, some voters blame the media, and especially the cable stations that jockey for position 24/7. Preston, a Trump supporter from Alabama, told me, "The media drives divisiveness hourly, and depending on what you watch, we have different truths. Fox and MSNBC can't get clicks and ads by being moderate, and this is a disaster for America." Jerry, a Democrat from New Hampshire, agreed with Preston, "I think that when we are scared or angry, we turn to the worst possible place: our biased news sources, featuring the talking heads who will make me feel better."

However, according to my panel of voters, what they believe to be the most dominant factor contributing to political divisiveness is that we, as a nation, have lost our ability to have conversations with people who are different from us, that we have lost our ability to listen to each other.

Nancy, an independent from Connecticut, believes "we are so rooted in individualism that we don't try to listen to each other's problems or walk in each other's shoes anymore." Allison, a Democrat from Wisconsin, said she longs for the days when we would respectfully debate politics. But now? "We have different opinions and so we decide not to talk about it—and not talking makes it worse."

Michelle, an independent from North Carolina, agrees. "Does anyone try and see the other side, or have we all become so close-minded that we have resorted to making fun of the other side or even disliking those who think differently? Everyone loves to speak and talk, but are they really listening?"

We all know what it's like to hear that the other side has done something outlandish yet again or to tune in to Rachel Maddow or Sean Hannity to satisfy our confirmation biases. We all see Americans screaming and yelling, and hiding behind anonymous comments on social media, not interested in trying to understand the other side. And, many of us have seen the TV experiments where experts bring people from both sides together for a day; Trump supporters and Trump detractors almost always leave hugging, "I had no idea!"

As our holiday season approaches, we might give listening another try. While Russian trolls do everything possible to pit us against one another, we can do more than wait for Congress to regulate the social media companies. Although we know that income inequality results in different lives and values and views of the world, we can do more than hope that tax or spending policies bring back a strong and vibrant middle class. We can break ourselves of the habit of retreating when we hear a comment with which we disagree, and learn how to have a dialogue again. We can say, "Tell me more" instead of "You are stupid and racist." Or, as Tim from Colorado told me, "We can get out from behind our phones, keyboards, and cameras and have a discussion over a beer, where we are less likely to say hurtful things."

It's time to do more than wake up, like Anna, with a pit in our stomachs. Jane, a Republican from Massachusetts, explains that "we need to stop complaining and start doing, to stop watching endless depressing news on TV and begin to revel in all that we have going for us." And Larry from Massachusetts reminds me about the late Senator John McCain's "Final Words to the Nation":[13] "We are 325 million opinionated, vociferous individuals . . . If only we remember that and give each other the benefit of the presumption that we all love our country, we will get through these challenging times."

Voters Are Disengaged with Foreign Policy

Foreign policy matters. When we make promises to a group like the Kurds that they should fight on our side in Syria—and then abandon them, as Trump did[14]—it makes everything harder in the future. It matters what we say when the leader of Saudi Arabia is implicated in the murder of a journalist.[15] It matters whether we behave as if Russia annexing parts of other nations is fine, or how we stand up to geopolitical competition from the Chinese autocracy.

Why does it matter? Because in the end, America is not alone in the world. We have to manage trade relationships and the value of our currency; after all, China owns a trillion dollars of US debt.[16] It matters when we need to work with other countries to push back on militaries that might threaten us or to rein in global warming. And we care about human rights all over the world.

These things are complicated to understand, and most of the action is taking place very far away from the day-to-day lives of American voters. From my conversations with Americans, I have learned foreign policy is inaccessible to them, and for many, it's boring. They are happy to comment on international issues, but their views tend to be superficial.

As a result, there is no area where a president has more leeway than in foreign policy: less pressure from voters, and at least in the recent past, fewer requirements for congressional approval of any actions a leader takes.

When Voters Hear about Foreign Policy, They Yawn

December 27, 2019 [17]

In a recent speech on foreign policy, former vice president Joe Biden was highly critical of President Trump, asserting that he has "bankrupted our credibility and alienated friends."[18] If you read the foreign policy platforms of most Democratic presidential candidates, their views are fairly similar. They all express an urgent need to restore America's moral leadership, to rebuild our alliances, and to regain our respect in the world.

Most voters don't care much, and that's a problem.

"Honestly, I am so far removed from all of this," said Michelle from North Carolina. "I am a new mom and just focused on trying to keep myself together, and I can't worry about Syria." Added Morgan from California, "My foreign policy creds are de minimis, but it seems that the issue with the Kurds has been going on for centuries—and so we should just stay out of it and worry about our own country."

When I asked my panel of 500 voters about foreign policy, most told me they don't have a lot to say, independent of educational levels or party affiliation. This is corroborated by a poll by Ipsos and FiveThirtyEight in which voters were asked about the issues most important to them in the 2020 presidential election.[19] Democrats overwhelmingly chose "ability to beat Trump," followed by health care, the economy, income inequality, and climate change. Foreign policy was not even in the top ten.

James, a Republican from Pennsylvania, put it to me in concrete terms: "I have relatives from South Philly who sent my cousin to West Chester University (about 30 miles away.) They packed a bag and stayed with my parents in Broomall to break up the trip. Do you think they know where Ukraine is?"

Sol Gittleman, my favorite professor from my days as a student at Tufts University, said in an interview that most Americans can't find Afghanistan on a map, no less Ukraine.

This is concerning because the president has significant freedom to act when it comes to our relationships and policies abroad. Whereas Congress can block domestic legislation, on the foreign front it mostly has only the power to declare war and ratify treaties. Thus, given that our president has enormous power when it comes to global issues, it should be more on voters' minds.

Even some Democrats who support Biden for president don't care much that 133 foreign affairs experts recently endorsed his candidacy.[20] As Shari from Delaware told me, "My friends and I like Biden mostly because he is a moderate, a steady hand, and a high-integrity individual, but I haven't really considered his foreign policy experience."

For many Trump supporters and some Democrats, the key to foreign policy seems to be hunkering down and staying out of the world's business. We have our own issues to worry about, said Alden, a Republican from Illinois. "Bring our guys home, let the Kurds deal with ISIS on their own, and let the other NATO countries pony up." Robert from Massachusetts said, "With our debt, we can no longer carry the rest of the world, even at the price of giving up our role as the undisputed global leader. It's the Trump doctrine."

This isolationist view and general lack of interest in world leadership is coloring how voters are thinking about impeachment. Although polls say that more than half of Americans wanted the president to be impeached,[21] most Americans are less engaged with the issue than they were last fall,[22] and the pundits are already talking about "impeachment fatigue." (The 13.8 million people who watched the impeachment proceedings represented a 31 percent drop from the number of viewers who watched when FBI Director James Comey testified[23] before the Senate Intelligence Committee.) The decision of the Democrats to focus narrowly on Ukraine may be partially to blame: An electorate that isn't passionate about foreign policy is relatively disengaged about who said what to whom in Ukraine—and it's not as spicy as a break-in at Watergate headquarters or a sexual liaison in the Oval Office.

The disinterest in foreign policy raises several questions: Can America really go it alone? Can our country be "great again" without knowing we can count on our allies? Can our economy be strong without the ability to leverage global markets? Can we address climate change without working across borders? Are walls and tariffs and isolation going to make Americans safer, happier, and more prosperous? Can we avoid terrorist attacks and war without a clear and experienced engagement with other countries?

Disengagement from the rest of the world may be dangerous, but Americans report that they are struggling to manage their own lives.[24] Nearly half do not have enough money set aside to cover expenses for three months, and 137 million say they are struggling to pay health care bills.[25] To them, a focus on the rest of the world is a luxury they cannot afford.

The Economy as a Key Issue for Everyone

I asked voters about the economy in March of 2020, when the coronavirus challenges had just begun. At the time, the economic outlook was pretty good, from low unemployment to low inflation to a booming stock market.

But economic news can turn in a hurry—and when it comes to downturns, it usually does. That's exactly what happened in the year after I published this: coronavirus shut things down, blew a hole in the employment numbers, and torpedoed consumer confidence. The market would likely have tanked as well if it hadn't been for the very generous and bipartisan Paycheck Protection Program and the tailwinds that the pandemic gave to technology companies, whose stocks soared in 2020.

Trump got a lot of the credit for a healthy economy in the first three years of his term. And although he got much of the blame for mishandling COVID, his insistence on keeping businesses open and getting people back to work—even when it risked their health—was perceived to be a positive to many voters; it signaled that the president was obsessed with the economy and jobs and helping small businesses.

Later in 2020, most of my voters gave Trump the win over Biden when it came to who would be most likely to bring the economy back after COVID. According to my data, this was a significant factor in why Donald Trump received more votes than the polls predicted.

Economic matters remain the factor most likely to change the minds of voters. Biden's success will most likely hinge on how he steers the nation back from the brink of disaster, much as Obama did in 2009. It's not a question of how you feel about the president and his politics. It's a question of how you feel about your job, your ability to make ends meet, and your future.

It's Still the Economy, Stupid

March 2, 2020[26]

What really matters as we think about the upcoming election? "The economy, stupid." That's how campaign strategist James Carville put it in 1992 when he was advising the Clinton campaign about what messages to focus on. Clearly, President Trump is also focused on the economy, calling ours the best it's ever been, and warning voters that their new-found prosperity will come to a halt if a Democrat wins the White House.

So, is the economy good or not? Well, it depends on who you ask. Most leading indicators are positive: in January, 225,000 jobs were added to the economy,[27] the unemployment rate was 3.6 percent, GDP growth was 2.1 percent, consumer confidence was high, building permits were up, interest rates were stable, and the stock market was on its way to hitting 30,000—at least until the recent coronavirus selloff. On the other hand, economists are starting to worry, and many Americans are working multiple jobs and taking out high-interest online installment loans[28] just to make ends meet. What really matters for November is not just the economy as an abstract concept or a series of metrics, but how actual Americans feel about it.

I asked my panel of 500 voters about the economy, just days before the coronavirus news came out. At that time, they all had similar answers to the following seven statements. How would you answer them? True or false?

1. I am personally experiencing the benefits of a good economy.

2. Millionaires should pay more in taxes.

3. I believe I pay my fair share of taxes.

4. Amazon should pay more in taxes.

5. I worry about how large the US deficit is.

6. The economy is only working for big corporations and the rich.

7. My health care costs have gone up significantly in the last year.

More than 85 percent of the respondents, from all along the political spectrum, gave the same answer to these questions. They responded "true" to all of the questions above except the last two, which 85 percent said were false.

It's striking how most people report they are benefiting from the current economy. Phil, a Republican from Boise, Idaho, reports that "my pay is up, my retirement funds are looking good, and my home value is up. And our local economy is doing great, with tons of jobs available for all who are looking for work." Alexis, a Democrat from Pennsylvania, adds, "In State College, the economy is booming. There's construction on three new luxury high-rise apartment buildings, and new stores seem to be popping up every week, with ads for jobs at nearly every store." And even Diana, a Republican from Iowa who lives near the poverty level, sees the benefits. She said, "For me, some of my monthly medical supplies went noticeably down last year. Some food prices went down, and, for a while, gas prices were down. Lots of sales seem to be going on, so when and if I buy items, I get them at a lower rate."

Deficits do weigh on voters. Andrew, an independent from Wisconsin, said, "I was disappointed when the Republicans, the party that boasts about being fiscally responsible, increased our deficit and therefore the rate at which the national debt is increasing." Andrew said he's also concerned because he believes we are borrowing from China to finance the deficit. "It seems as though we are trying to just hand superpower status to China."

And there is barely a voter on my panel who thinks they should pay more in taxes.

On the other hand, Republicans and Democrats are split on three of the true/false questions.

1. I worry that the economy will take a bad turn in the next nine months.

2. I give former President Obama much of the credit for the good economy.

3. Income inequality is a huge problem in the United States.

Democrats are more concerned about the future, credit Obama for at least part of the good economy, and believe that income inequality is a massive problem. Republicans tend to be bullish on the future (as long as Trump stays in office), give

Trump full credit for the current economy, and are indifferent to the gap between the rich and the poor.

"My IRA account has been growing with the trajectory of the stock market," said Catherine, a Democrat from Massachusetts, "but I am afraid to invest for the long term because I fear volatility and market collapse." Lawrence, a Democrat from Boston, added, "We are creating a nation of renters, who live paycheck to paycheck, with little saved for retirement, and unable to pay a major emergency expense. Income inequality is a huge problem, and it simmers below the surface of our economy and our society."

Republicans are more optimistic, and they believe that income inequality is solvable. Peter from Illinois doesn't see wealth as a zero-sum game. "As the 1 percent get richer, it doesn't mean they are taking it from the pockets of the bottom 50 percent."

This kind of voter sentiment raises a key issue for Democrats. In the absence of a recession or a precipitous drop in the stock market, most electoral models, such as those by Moody's analytics, predict a Trump victory. Clearly, if the stock market downturn from the coronavirus continues, all bets could be off. For now, Democrats are challenged to respond in a compelling way to a president whose message is: You may not like me, but you have to vote for me because if you elect the other guys, say goodbye to the economy you love!

What won't work in a general election is to communicate that the economy is bad or that it is working for only those at the top, because this just does not match with the experience of most voters. Even more, a message about completely overhauling our health care system—or dramatically increasing taxes to pay for more entitlements—is unlikely to generate significant support.

What could resonate? Democrats could win, not by denying that we have a robust economy, but by showing how our good economy could be even better if rich individuals and corporations paid their fair share, just as everyday Americans do—or that our good economy won't last forever, as people borrow too much at high interest rates, and pay more and more for rent. They could also point out how dependent our good economy is on a healthy global economy—with strong markets for American products and reliable sources of vital raw materials and supplies, and with a worldwide commitment to working together on everything from disease to climate issues.

Clearly a continued coronavirus scare, with its negative impact on the economy, potentially eliminates Trump's most powerful talking point. And above and beyond the economy is the critical reminder that we are all experiencing how interconnected our world is—an important talking point for the Democrats.

No matter what, it's clear that when it comes to the economy, the Democrats have not yet created a message—or a plan—that will motivate voters to shift how they think about their pocketbooks. Perception is everything, and right now, if it's the economy, stupid, it's time for some candidate to get smart.

Abortion: Moral Viewpoints and Practical Challenges

Written for this book in February 2021.

"Can we talk?" Jimmy wrote in the email. He was an Alabama Republican who had participated in my research project weekly since 2016. Jimmy explained, "Today was the worst day of my life and I'd rather tell you about it on the phone."

I dialed his number, wondering how someone who was typically calm and steady could be so upset. Jimmy was a 40-year-old car mechanic, married with two children, and it was unlike him to exaggerate.

"Jimmy, what happened?"

"My 15-year-old daughter got an abortion today. We prayed about it all weekend, and we decided as a family that it was the best option."

This truly shocked me. You see, Jimmy was a devout Christian, a dedicated pro-lifer, happy with President Trump and all he stood for. During my first conversation with him, he told me that he didn't understand liberals, and he couldn't fathom how anyone could be pro-choice.

"Oh, Jimmy," I responded. "I don't know what to say."

"I know what you're thinking," he replied. "But here's the thing. She made a mistake with a young man one evening, but the decision to have the abortion took us many evenings of talking about it. It feels like a death."

"I hear you."

"It's different from the pro-choice people who don't see it as a big deal."

It was not appropriate at that moment for me to tell Jimmy that he had an incorrect perception of those pro-choice people. But as we talked, I realized that his perception drove so much of what he felt. He saw liberal women as cavalier about abortion: not taking it seriously, using it as birth control, and unable to acknowledge that there was the beginning of a life at stake. His perception that "pro-choice" meant "casual about abortion" drove all of his anger about the issue.

There are few voter issues that are more polarizing than the issue of whether it is moral to terminate a pregnancy. Abortion may be the most emotional issue voters have—so much so that nearly one third of my voters told me that they would never vote for a candidate on the other side of the fence. Those pro-choice voters tell me they would not vote for a pro-life candidate even if they agree with that candidate on every other issue. And on the pro-life side, there are many single-issue voters who will vote for a candidate they completely disagree with if that candidate is pro-life.

David, an evangelical Christian from Michigan, told me, "The people in my church saw Trump as a Messiah figure who was going to rescue us over the Obama years of gay marriage, pro-choice, and more. We were literally told that if we didn't vote for Trump, we would have the blood of murdered unborn babies in our hands."

Despite David's concern over "the way Trump lived his life," David thus voted for him in November of 2016.

Mary, a Democrat from North Carolina, feels the opposite way. She praised the services of Planned Parenthood, which helped her get birth control, counseled her about safe sex, and provided medical services earlier in her life. And, she said, "I am terrified that some white man in his seventies will dictate whether or not a woman can have an abortion."

Once again, there are misconceptions about elements of how the other side feels. Time and again, pro-life voters echoed Jimmy, telling me that pro-choice women took abortion lightly, making a fast decision without consulting family members, and believing that they could get as many abortions as they wanted. The notion that a pro-choice voter would see abortion as an excruciating decision was incomprehensible to them—just as it is difficult for pro-choice voters to imagine that someone like Jimmy would allow his daughter to end her teenage pregnancy.

We are grappling not with the issue of abortion, but with a caricature of the attitudes about it. Democrats don't approve of killing babies without consideration, regardless of what conservatives may say. Republicans don't think women's bodies are the property of the state, even if that's how the liberal talking points frame it. The truth is something like what happened in Jimmy's brain—a frequently painful decision for which either alternative falls between intensely unpleasant and unthinkable.

This is not an area where we have clear common ground, but both sides would be better off if we adopted policies that would make abortion as rare as possible: better education about sex, easier access to birth control, and counseling with a heart. But it may not be possible to imagine a politician who could talk about it without committing political suicide.

Part III

Voters and Their Passion for Character

Wwe like to think that the character of our candidates makes a great deal of difference in who we vote for. But my conversations with voters reveal that the truth is far more complicated.

It is certainly accurate that Donald Trump redefined the way we think about presidents, with a far more direct, unvarnished, and combative style that defied presidential norms. But as my voters told me, acting "presidential" is not just about being polite and making soaring speeches.

Instead, I found that character is sometimes about how dogged a president is in defending the ideals for which he was elected, which Trump voters felt he did quite well. It often seemed as if voters projected character onto whatever candidate matched their political outlook, rather than watching behavior and deciding dispassionately.

Politics now plays out against a backdrop where every candidate must fend off accusations of corruption, and where it's increasingly difficult to sort out truth from lies in a partisan media environment. If they're all corrupt—or are perceived that way—then voters pick the candidate that they like, regardless of the claims of corruption.

Given that the partisan accusations are not slowing down, we may never see another candidate who isn't painted as corrupt. In such a world, voters will still devise their own blueprints for how they think about character. They will ask the fundamental questions: Does this person understand people like me? Will the candidate advocate for the things I care about? Can I trust this person? Will this person keep me and my family safe and treated fairly? According to my voters across the political spectrum, these questions will always be front and center as they think about who they want as leaders.

The President's Outrageous Behavior

By violating the norms of how a president should behave—and how a president should communicate—Donald Trump challenged everything about the way we conduct politics in America.

In 2018, it was his privately captured statements about "shithole countries." But with Trump, the next violation was always just around the corner.

The pattern I described in this op-ed would be repeated over and over throughout Trump's term. My voters didn't think it mattered. His insults were just more red meat to get outraged about, full of sound and fury and signifying…not much.

The Insults of Our President

January 15, 2018 [1]

Once again, our news cycle is dominated by President Trump's latest comments, this time about "shithole countries."

My voters across the political spectrum have responded with words like "disgusting," "inflammatory," and "shameful." However, while liberals are using that language to describe the president, the Trump base is using the same words to talk about the media.

"Does our president have any decency at all?" asked Monroe, a Democrat from Mississippi.

"We have reached a new low," moaned Bernice, a Democrat from Oklahoma. "I have posted my apology on Facebook to all groups, races, and countries he has insulted, and I am utterly disgusted that those in his party are not outraged as well."

On the other hand, Eve, a Republican from Ohio, told me, "I am disgusted over this constant effort by the media to destroy this presidency." Added Kevin from Arizona, "Come on. The only thing that bothers me is the holier-than-thou media reaction, as they try to broadcast his words and send the country into a tizzy." In general, Trump voters say they are happy with the president's policies, and are focused on what he does instead of what he says.

Most striking to me is the déjà vu. Trump says something completely unacceptable, Democrats are outraged, and the president's comments take over the airwaves for several days, distracting us from the issues of the day. We have heard more about his bigoted rant than a false missile alert in Hawaii, the fear that Dreamers have about being deported, the continued devastation in Puerto Rico, the vulnerability of the Iran nuclear agreement, and so much more.

As Corey, a Republican from New Hampshire, wrote me, "Trump said something disgusting. What else is new? Are we serious that we didn't see this coming?"

If we believe that it is critical for the president of the United States to be a model of dignified behavior for our children, a beacon for the rest of the world, and someone whose comments make us feel proud to be Americans, Trump will continue to disappoint us. If we thought that Trump would mature as he learned the job, that he would evolve and become more diplomatic, we have learned that this won't happen. The question becomes how we deal with it, especially when our outrage is not making much of a difference. Perhaps next time the president says something offensive, we can collectively decide not to dignify his comments with a response.

How We See the Washington Swamp

The term "drain the swamp" has been used by political leaders for decades. Ronald Reagan, for instance, used the term in 1982 when he created The Grace Commission to eliminate wasteful spending in the federal government.[2] But no one embraced the term as much as Donald Trump, who tweeted it 79 times in the three weeks before the 2016 election. "Drain the swamp" was a brilliant campaign slogan for an outsider coming to Washington, signifying that corruption and government were inseparable.

Voters from all ends of the political spectrum agreed that swamp-draining was a worthy and important mission. They saw Washington as a place where people come to get special favors, inside deals, undeserved appointments, and secret cash payments. Many who voted for Trump told me that the slogan was more compelling for them than "Make America Great Again."

It was clear then—and it still is now—that corruption outrages voters. Of course, each side is convinced that dirty, rotten scoundrels are the other guys.

The Muck and Mud in Washington— How Voters See It

February 7, 2018[3]

"I hated almost everything about Donald Trump during election season," said John from Nevada. "There was only one exception, and that was his slogan about draining the swamp. I thought that was really important."

In my conversations with diverse and divided voters, there is one issue that Americans agree on more than any other: the need to drain the swamp. Politicians from Ronald Reagan to Nancy Pelosi have used that term to decry the Washington morass, and both Trump and Senator Bernie Sanders made fixing the rigged system a central message of their campaigns. Voters from across the political spectrum describe Washington as rife with greed, grift, and bureaucracy, reminiscent of a bog full of disease-carrying mosquitoes. They believe it's time to drain that swamp, and they all want pretty much the same thing when they say that.

"To me, draining the swamp is about taking big money out of congressional decisions," said Maria, a Democrat from South Carolina. "We need to take away this web of deceit, eye-winking, handshaking, and you-scratch-my-back/I'll-scratch-yours." Nearly 80 percent of voters in my panel bemoan the outsize influence of the rich, the NRA, pharmaceutical companies, and especially lobbyists, whose activity surged to $3.34 billion last year.

Voters also believe that our government is bureaucratic and wasteful, no longer responsive to the needs of constituents. As Desiree, a millennial Democrat from New Hampshire, told me, "The idea that DC has many people that are just there for power and not for the people rings so true for me!" Jasmine, a Republican from Maine, agreed: "The people who are in government should be there for the people, and not be career politicians that cozy up to lobbyists, line their pockets, and make deals to further their careers. They should do what is really right rather than what is right for them personally."

Voters cited dozens of examples. Lisa, a Republican from Georgia, talked about the waste and power plays she sees daily in her government job. Lynn, an independent from North Carolina, shared stories of FEMA giving people $500 after a Category One storm, simply because they claimed they lost a freezer full of groceries. Others cited Bob Corker, who entered Congress deeply in debt and is now worth nearly $70 million, allegedly because he traded on inside information while serving on the Senate Banking Committee. Said Robert, a Republican from Mississippi, "I don't think our Founding Fathers ever intended anyone to be in office for 30 or 40 years or to become millionaires in the process."

And most Democratic and Republican voters also agree on one other thing: Trump not only hasn't drained the swamp, he may be making things worse.

"I am a Trump supporter for sure," said Jose, a Republican from California, "but on a scale of 1 to 10, I give him a 2 for draining the swamp. It was compelling to me to have an outsider go in and blow everything up, but the only progress in that area so far is in sexual harassment and assault, and we obviously can't give him credit for that." Added Joseph, a Republican from Arizona, "I am happy to have more money in my paycheck, but the people who are really benefiting are the rich people. I mean, they didn't even change the tax rate on carried interest [in the recently passed tax plan]."

Many perceive Trump's cabinet appointments as making the swamp even more corrupt. "Trump thought that draining the swamp was about bringing in new blood, and instead we got a bunch of Goldman Sachs executives and other rich people who are adding to the goo," said Jenny, a Democrat from Iowa. Voters reminded me of the stories about expensive flights taken by cabinet secretaries, and bemoan what they believe is just a new group of cronies who are beholden to new special interests.

For now, the swamp drama continues. Democrats will decry Trump's unwillingness to divest his business interests or implement Congress's sanctions on Russia. Republicans will hold up the recently declassified Devin Nunes memo as evidence that even the FBI is tainted. What Trump has shown voters—at least so far—is that just because he is a blustering outsider, it doesn't mean he has the competence to take on the distrust people have for Washington. The hunger for brave and unsullied candidates with both the guts and the intelligence to change the system has not died. This is an opportunity for new leaders who, knowing that we are up to our necks in alligators, can bring back confidence in our democracy.

Character as a Candidate's Most Important Quality

I f you want to get folks talking, ask them what it means for someone to be "presidential." Most people will respond with their views on character and how important it is. During the 2020 presidential campaign, it was most striking to me that voters continually expressed admiration for the personal qualities of their preferred candidate. You might not like Trump, but his supporters marveled at his strength and conviction. You might not like Biden, but his supporters applauded his personal story of courage and compassion.

I believe character will always be a dominant issue on the ballot. We want our leaders to reflect our own values and life lessons, and as I spoke to voters across the country in 2019, this was their crystal-clear conviction.

Does Trump's Character Count?

June 9, 2019[4]

Stop any Democrat on the street these days and ask them about the most important quality they look for in a president, and you will hear about character. As Cara, a Democrat from South Carolina, explains to me, "Our president needs to be an example of America's best values—to us and to the rest of the world." When it comes to how they assess a president, 95 percent of the Democrats in my panel of 500 voters rate "character and integrity" a 10 on a ten-point scale.

It has been more than 50 years since Martin Luther King Jr. talked about his dream that one day his children "will not be judged by the color of their skin but by the content of their character." Looking back from the perspective of over half a century, do we know what that quality actually is and how much it matters?

Cathy from Massachusetts thinks it is clearly evident that President Trump's character is a problem. "This is the first president in my memory who has operated without a shred of decency, with no guiding principle other than greed and self-interest," she says. Most Democrats I speak with have similar sentiments.

There are Republicans in my sample who feel the same way. Peter from Illinois voted for John McCain and Mitt Romney for president, but wrote in John Kasich's name in 2016, mostly because of what he saw as Trump's defective character. "Our president is a petty, narcissistic, loathsome, sociopathic excuse for a human being," he tells me.

Here's the rub. Last week I also asked Trump voters to rate how important character and integrity are for a president. After two and a half years of conversations with these voters, my expectation was that character would be a "nice to have," and certainly not as important to Trump's base as the progress they believe he has made on their key issues, such as the economy. However, on a scale of one to 10, with 10 signifying "extremely important," the average for the group was 8.25, and many of Trump's most ardent supporters rated this quality a 10. They see character and integrity as critical. What's going on here?

"You can judge character in many ways," says Susan, a Republican from Ohio who supports the president. Like many Trump fans, she is not happy with the president's behavior, but she believes that he is dealing with a swampy, corrupt federal government. "He's bold and unorthodox and courageous in his methods and I frankly love it. It's high time DC was awakened," she stated. Brenda from Pennsylvania agrees. "This is a man who is totally committed to what he believes in," she tells me. "Even in the face of constant opposition from the media and from the Democrats, he forges ahead, and I admire that quality." Jim, a Trump enthusiast from Nebraska, invokes Maya Angelou when talking about Trump's character: you may encounter many defeats, but you must not be defeated. Time and again, Trump supporters rate their president high on integrity because they believe he does what he says he is going to do.

Trump supporters also say they have no alternative. Some believe that the president is no worse than many other past occupants of the White House, and they ultimately voted for him because, as Cynthia from Massachusetts declares, "Hillary Clinton was certainly not the beacon of character and integrity, so what were we to do?"

So, while character and integrity to these voters is important, it is more nuanced, and it is relative. If an alternative candidate has good character but is a socialist, they will vote for Trump. If a new candidate has good character but believes in open borders or third-trimester abortion, they will vote for the reelection of the president.

Robert, a Republican from New York, offers his "Christian view" that the measure of character is whether the person strives to remain without sin. "The president represents all of us ... and other nations must be able to take us at our word without a moment of doubt." Although he believes character is a vitally important quality, he sees no one in the government today meeting that standard.

As we listen to the 23 Democratic candidates for president talk about why they are running, it's striking that most talk about our moment in history: that defeating Donald Trump, a man of terrible character, is a national imperative. The stakes seem higher with the publishing of the Mueller report, in that most Democrats believe the conclusions dig an even deeper hole when it comes to the president's integrity.

The message from my panel, however, is clear: the "bad character" message is insufficient for a Democratic win in 2020. This is especially important as we look at the president's approval ratings, which are hovering in the low 40 percent range.[5] If what voters tell me is true, low approval numbers won't necessarily translate into a vote against Trump in 2020; we can imagine voters who disapprove of the president's lies, tweets, or his name calling, but who will still cast their vote for him because they have a different definition of character and integrity. (And moreover, of the 500 voters I surveyed, only nine report having read the Mueller report.)

Jane Eyre, the heroine of the famous Charlotte Brontë novel, stated, "I am not an angel, and I will not be one 'til I die," and we cheered as she said it. Trump may be no angel, but in 2020, disapproving Americans just might vote for him anyway.

Joe Biden's Real Advantage: His Humanity

In the summer of 2018, it was far from clear who would win the Democratic nomination for president, with dozens of candidates either declared or waiting in the wings.

But if you had listened to my voters, you would have seen clues, not only to the winner of the Democratic nomination but to the eventual election of the president.

The media never tires of focusing on the extremes and the tensions within political parties. President Trump thrived in this environment, which magnified his volatility and kept him in the spotlight. But voters—including those who identify as Republicans—would eventually become fatigued and long for stability.

Despite Biden's age and lack of flash, his brand, from the beginning, was one of a mature, compassionate man who had been through tremendous tragedy in his own life—and who would know how to build trust with everyday Americans. It was a contrast to Trump, and a major factor behind why a wide variety of Democrats and a sufficient number of Republicans backed him to generate a 7-million-vote edge in the popular vote.

Joe Biden's Humanity Could Be His Edge in 2020

August 9, 2018[6]

Ever since Donald Trump's presidency hit the 500-day mark, the media have been speculating daily about the next presidential election. As we watch the ongoing reality show, November 3, 2020, seems like it will be the final episode of a multiyear season of *Washington Survivor*.

Which Democrat will rise above the pack? A few weeks ago, CNN published its ranking of the Democrats most likely to be the nominee, based on polling and lessons from history.[7] In reverse order of likelihood, as of the end of July, they are:

> Senator Sherrod Brown of Ohio;
> Former New Orleans mayor Mitch Landrieu;
> Senator Cory Booker of New Jersey;
> Governor Steve Bullock of Montana;
> Former attorney general Eric Holder;
> Senator Bernie Sanders of Vermont;
> Senator Kirsten Gillibrand of New York;
> Senator Kamala Harris of California;
> Senator Elizabeth Warren of Massachusetts;
> Former vice president Joe Biden.

Regardless of what you think of this list (why are former Massachusetts governor Deval Patrick and Mayor Eric Garcetti of Los Angeles missing?), what would my panel of 500 voters think of it?

Half the group had no idea who Brown, Landrieu, Booker, and Bullock are. Only three candidates were known to all: Biden, Warren, and Sanders. And the favorite, far ahead of the rest, and palatable even to many Republicans: Joe Biden.

Some voters talked about Facebook posts about him, while others had read his recent book, *Promise Me, Dad*. Some talked about his ability to connect with working-class voters, while others talked about his foreign policy experience. Sharleen, an African-American from Virginia, admitted that despite her commitment to getting women and people of color elected, she would be "down for Biden," and Chas, a white coal miner from Kentucky, said that he trusts that Biden supports the troops in a profound way because of the tragic loss of his son Beau.[8]

The theme from Democrats is that Biden is less extreme than the others on the list and has the potential to heal the division in our country, to "tap into the humanity of everyone." Said Tim from Wyoming, "I am scared to death that the Democrat reaction to this crazy time will be to nominate a super left-wing, socialist-leaning candidate, who will ultimately get massacred by Trump and only make our divisions worse." Brenda from Michigan added, "Biden has friends on both sides of the aisle and is one of the few on the list who has publicly demonstrated an ability to appear bipartisan, and in the coming election, that will become incredibly important."

Many Republicans—including many Trump voters—said they could live with Biden. Said Carly from New Hampshire, "If Biden were running, I would watch the debates very carefully and give him a fair shake." She explained that he is pro-military, pro-ICE, and pro-police, and that she doesn't believe he is corrupt. Added Jesse from Texas, "If I woke up tomorrow and Biden was president, I'd be thankful it was him and none of the others on the list." Many Republicans admitted that they would have voted for Biden in 2016 if he were the nominee.

The dominant theme about Biden from across the political spectrum was how people feel about him as a person. Over 40 of my voters described him using the word "love." Voters talked about his "class," "dignity," "inner strength," "patriotism," "authenticity," "compassion," and his ability to "stop the boat from rocking violently and to lead us back to some sense of normalcy and decency."

The primary negative for Biden is that he is 75 years old. "I would want a presidential candidate in her fifties or sixties, mostly due to the rigors of campaigning," said Richard from Connecticut. "However, I'd make an exception for Biden."

Voters under 30 were the ones who had the least concern about age. They wrote that health and stamina are more important than age, that it wasn't an issue with Bernie Sanders, and that being president doesn't require the rigors of playing football. "For what it's worth," said Joey from New York, "I've always had the impression that I'll live to at least 100, and I can't really imagine wanting to retire before 80."

When I pressed on the age issue, voters mostly believe that 80 might be the new 60. After all, 85-year-old Justice Ruth Bader Ginsburg says she has five more years on the Supreme Court;[9] investor Warren Buffett is 87 and starting a new health care company;[10] and Patriots quarterback Tom Brady, who just turned 41, can take hits and still throw accurate touchdown passes. Ira from California, who is 83, said that he feels 60, swims 50 laps a day followed by an hour at the gym, and writes and sculpts to stay sharp; he would consider Biden if he thought he hadn't "lost his fastball." Said Pete, a Massachusetts college student, "My logic says he is too old and the party needs new blood. But I love Joe

Biden as a politician and as a human being. So as for Joe Biden running, my brain says no, but my heart says, 'I'm all in. When do you need me to start knocking on doors, Joe?'"

The lack of name recognition for the other candidates will change, of course, in the next two years. But just as the name Trump was an advantage in a variegated field of 17 Republicans in 2016, Biden's familiarity could be a huge asset among a large slate of candidates.

Democrats could lurch to the left in 2020, backing a candidate intended to swing the political world back from four Republican-dominated years. No milquetoast moderate is likely to win the nomination. But a Democrat who can actually win in 2020 will have to unite the party with liberal bona fides, appeal to those across the aisle, and promise to normalize a government reeling from Trumpian chaos. That sounds a lot like Joe Biden.

Lies on All Sides

One year before the 2020 election, I asked voters about integrity. We were in the midst of the first impeachment inquiry, which focused on Trump's alleged corrupt outreach to the president of Ukraine. We were also awash in questions about Hunter Biden's activities in Ukraine as a director of an oil company there.

The key questions for voters focused on how they felt about a leader who was unscrupulous. And the unfortunate answer seemed to be: they're all corrupt, and they all lie. Republicans felt there was little difference in the malfeasance on either side, while Democrats, even though they were suspicious of everyone in Washington, felt that Republican candidates were worse.

There have been so many accusations of crooked behavior in recent presidential politics that the litany of accusations has become the backdrop of every contest. Negative advertising, partisan media, and Twitter attacks inflame these sentiments. And, to a certain extent, they cancel each other out.

This is especially frustrating to Democrats, who watched as the *Washington Post* tracked President Trump's lies, totaling 30,573 by the end of his term.[11] It seemed to them that an average of 20 lies per day was not the same as "I did not have sexual relations with that woman" (referring to former president Bill Clinton's claims in 1998 about his affair with intern Monica Lewinsky).

You might think that voters would choose the candidate who is less bad and avoid the one who appears most corrupt. But when the decision looks like that, many voters fall back on ideology and party identification to make their decision. The reasoning: "If they're all sleazy, I'd rather have my guy than the other one."

As I write this, the same "they're all liars" question is playing out in Texas. The state is suffering a deep freeze, and many residents are without power or clean water. Democrats say it's due to poor planning and natural gas pipelines and plants failing. Republicans, including the governor, blame it on frozen wind turbines. When you're shivering in the dark, it's pretty hard to figure out who's lying and who's just manipulating the situation.

It may be a forlorn hope that we'll have cleaner-looking candidates in the future, or that their character and past behavior will actually determine who wins. It's more likely to be just one of a stew of elements that matter. Voters will have to work harder to figure out which accusations are valid and which are just a smokescreen.

Playing the Integrity Card
November 1, 2019 [12]

"The lying just makes me crazy," said Justin, a Republican from Pennsylvania. "I can't figure out how he can constantly deny his guilt when we all know how his family has profited from his position. He's just another elite—and, it's clear to me that he will not be our president after the next election."

Justin was talking about former vice president Joe Biden.

In speaking with my panel of 500 American voters over the last three years, I have tried to maintain an objective posture, but I had to bite. "Really?" I blurted out. "You think the dishonesty problem is with Biden and not Trump?"

"They are all unethical," said Justin. "Welcome to the United States of America and how you can get rich by being an elected official."

Liz, a Republican from Oregon, agreed. "I thought Biden might just be a regular guy, but now it's clear to me that he is just one more elite who is pretending to be like us." Justin and Liz are both confident President Trump will win a second term.

I asked my panel to predict the outcome of the 2020 presidential election, and to help me understand what events would occur between now and then. There were many common themes: Trump will be impeached by the House, but the Senate will not remove him; no significant challenger to the president will emerge on the Republican side; and the country will become more divided than ever leading up to the election. There was no agreement on the likely Democratic candidate, but most of the chatter was about Joe Biden and Elizabeth Warren.

The most salient idea on which they agreed is that Washington is a sea of dishonesty, and that our politics are sleazy. The key difference is that Republicans tend to apply this notion to both parties, while Democrats tend to believe it's just the other guys.

Most Republicans from my group—and especially those who support Trump—are convinced that people who enter politics these days sell their souls to the devil, put themselves above those they represent, and end up getting rich in the process. They are convinced that the other side is often corrupt and hypocritical—and this belief colors their thinking about who they support and why.

Supporting a flawed politician like Trump then becomes easier for them, because if everybody is self-centered and shady, it's easier to support the flawed politician whose policies you agree with.

Trump supporters don't like it that the president profits from his presidency, but they don't see him as the first to make money as a result of his position. Said Arlene from Texas, "Hillary Clinton claimed that she and Bill were 'dead broke' when they left the White House, and yet last time I checked, they were worth $45 million.[13] The Obamas talk about the South Side of Chicago, but they now own an $8 million mansion in Georgetown,[14] and just bought a $15 million mansion in Martha's Vineyard."[15]

Thus, Republicans give Trump a hall pass; he is a bad dude, but he is their bad dude. And they are confident that he will prevail in November 2020. When we wonder why anyone would vote for Donald Trump in 2020, most Republicans say there is no one on the Democratic debate stage who appeals to them. This narrative about corruption is often dominant: they believe that the other side is dishonest and, even worse, has a holier-than-thou attitude about integrity.

Most Democrats see it differently. They see their own party as principled and forthright, and they yearn for a return to the days when they felt proud of the ethics in the White House. They are hopeful that Trump's deeds and words will end his presidency by inauguration day.

The issues abound: a quid pro quo in Ukraine, Trump's insistence that there was nothing wrong with hosting the G7 at his Doral Hotel, his questionable partnership with Rudy Giuliani, and the presidential "lie count" exceeding 13,435.

"I will vote for any of the Democrats if they are going against Trump," said Caren from California. "He is the most corrupt president in our history, and when I hear it has spread to the Justice Department, it actually scares me."

When Trump supporters hear that, they laugh: wake up to the reality in Washington.

Although Democrats don't agree that all politicians are dishonest, they are drawn to the broader message about a rigged and unfair system. Both Democrats and Republicans talk about the class of people in our country who continually have an unfair advantage: a connection, a friend in power, a special deal. They see it in the college admissions scandal, in the ability of rich criminals to get light sentences, and in the benefits that accrue to family members of politicians with famous names. They detest not just the lack of a level playing field, but the frequent insistence by these elites that they are regular people who care deeply about the "regular citizens" of America.

As Democrats scream, "What about Ivanka?," Republicans say, "What about Hunter?" When Democrats scream, "What about the Saudis staying in the Trump Hotel?," Republicans respond, "What about Clinton selling out the Lincoln Bedroom?" The Democrats scream, "Mitch McConnell is biased and obstructionist at every turn," and the Republicans respond, "The Democrats are running the impeachment inquiry in an unbelievably unfair way."[16] And so on.

Politicians who will succeed in this sleaze-weary environment must walk in the shoes of people who resent the unfairness they perceive in their lives. We can all relate to the nauseating feeling we have when we think about a father paying money to have his son depicted as an international water polo star in return for admission to the University of Southern California.[17] The people who are least surprised about this case include both Trump supporters and those who are donating to the left wing of the Democratic Party, who see an entire class of Americans metaphorically taking water polo photos on a daily basis.

Claiming that you are cleaner than your sleazy opponents is unlikely to extend anyone's appeal beyond his or her political base. Any Democrat who hopes to win must inspire worn-out voters with a message that goes beyond "Trump is a bad guy." Competence, inspiration, and ideas that address an unfair system have a chance here. But, contrary to what we hear on a daily basis, playing the integrity card, however justified, won't change the outcome we all experienced in 2016.

Masks, Freedom, and Compassion

The death toll in the United States from the coronavirus in 2020 and 2021 has topped half a million people. And yet, during the pandemic, the question of how to protect yourself from contagion was positioned, like everything else, as a partisan issue.

I admit I used to walk down the street in 2020 and make bets on the political party of people who passed me, just based on whether they were wearing a mask. But when I talked to voters about it in the middle of that year, only the most extreme were completely rejecting the advice to wear a mask. People were also making up their own rules about safe behavior, which was to be expected in the face of general and ever-shifting advice from medical professionals, not to mention different rules for different states.

Although character is a major factor for Americans when they think about who they want as leaders, it is also an important factor in how we think about each other. For instance, the character of a maskless person in a pandemic might be suspect because it looks like they are flaunting their lack of concern for others. Mask-wearing is the perfect instance of how we draw conclusions about the character of someone we don't even know. I was certainly guilty of this in the summer of 2020—until I decided to interview people strolling along Boston's Harborwalk.

Who Are the Maskless People?

August 3, 2020 [18]

In June, a shopper in North Hollywood, California, was confronted at a Trader Joe's for not wearing a mask. Her diatribe about "Democratic Pigs" went viral[19]—and so did a July 19 video showing American Airlines passengers applauding as a woman who refused to wear a mask[20] was booted from a flight.

Wearing a face covering has the support of public health officials. Just last week, Dr. Anthony Fauci, director of the National Institute of Allergy and Infectious Diseases, urged government leaders to be "as forceful as possible" about wearing face masks, no matter where they live, to ward off the spread of COVID-19.[21] We wear masks to protect ourselves and those around us, given that asymptomatic or pre-symptomatic citizens can be contagious.

Who are these maskless people? A recent Gallup poll concluded that people who refused to wear a mask were more likely to be Republicans.[22] Could it be true that more than a third of Republicans are ignoring a government directive to don a mask?

When I consider those in my panel of 500 voters who are undoubtedly part of President Trump's base, Brenna is one who comes to mind. A dedicated bus driver for a Pennsylvania school district, she believes that Trump is the best president we have ever had, and she is satisfied with how he is managing the pandemic. She fits the profile of a "mask rejector."

Instead, she told me she wears a mask often: "When I go into a store, I wear a mask, and when I return to work, I will be wearing one all the time. You can bet you won't be seeing me at a concert, ball game, or any other large gathering."

Or take Kevin, a college professor from North Carolina who holds Trump in high esteem. On a scale of 1 to 10, with 10 meaning "I wear a mask all the time," and 1 meaning "I don't own one," Kevin rated himself a 7. Over time, he has become convinced that when he wears a mask, he is protecting his neighbors. "Two months ago, if you told me to wear a mask, I would have told you something that you can't print in your newspaper," he said, "but now I think it might help, and I am willing to do anything reasonable to get this overblown COVID behind us."

Brenna and Kevin are not alone. Over 90 percent of my panel of voters rated themselves a 7 or higher when asked about wearing a mask. They don't necessarily like it, complaining about heat, difficulty breathing, and discomfort, but they report that they are mostly in compliance and are unhappy with those who are not. Said Phil, a Republican from Idaho, "I'm very disappointed in people that don't wear a mask. I think they're rude, uncaring people that I want nothing to do with."

The minuscule group of voters in my panel who reported that they rarely wear masks said they were rejecting government overreach, valuing their freedom above all else. And, yes, a few thought the coronavirus was a hoax.

We tend to make assumptions about those we see with no face covering: that they are irresponsible, uneducated, or just selfish. Last Tuesday, I stopped several unmasked walkers on the Boston Harborwalk—all under age 35—and, like my panel, most claimed to be rigorous about wearing a mask. They profess to be compliant when inside—and, when outdoors, they believe they can create enough social distance to be safe. Said Marci, who lives in the North End, "My friends and I basically make a judgment call about the level of contagion. If we are going to be outside and it's mostly open, we leave our masks at home." Added her friend Emily, "If I think I am going to violate the 6-foot rule only for a few seconds, I don't think a mask is warranted."

What can we infer from the data? First, in the absence of clear guidelines, which vary from state to state, people are inventing their own rules. I've heard about the "2/3 Rule," implying that you should always do two of the following: go outside, wear a mask, and practice social distancing. I also heard the "Ask the Host Rule," the "How Fast You Are Moving Rule," and the "Look at Your Local Outbreak Rule." Second, people's behavior doesn't always mirror their commitment. Third, those videos of noncompliant rebels we see every day make for fascinating viewing, but to assume that mask rejectors are running rampant throughout our country distorts reality.

In some ways, it is a relief to know that when I see someone's face totally exposed, they might not be flaunting their politics but just making the best judgment call they can.

Both President Trump and Senate majority leader Mitch McConnell recently changed their tune and came out in favor of masks, signaling to supporters that a bare face is not a requirement for advertising your devotion to the president.[23] A great public service announcement with more precise guidelines could help the problem—especially if religious leaders, conservative governors, right-leaning media, and the president start signaling that it's the patriotic thing to do.

We can take comfort in knowing that most Americans are getting with the program. They are dealing with the sweat, the annoyance, and the foggy glasses, and they have no plans to run through your grocery store screaming about their liberty. The danger is not from those who have chosen to politicize masks.

It's from Americans who, in the absence of more specific and clear direction from our leaders, have had to fill the information vacuum about best practices.

This is an anxious time for Americans. The COVID-19 tests are not always accurate; the science is evolving; the data are inconsistent; and the guidance keeps changing. We need scientists and government officials to give us their best—and more precise— shot. In the meantime, they are delegating the details to a group of amateur public health experts: the citizens of America.

Part IV

How Political Culture Inflames Our Tensions

There was a time when most of us read the same newspapers, watched the same few TV stations, and formed our opinions in the same shared environment. We still had plenty of things to disagree about, but those disagreements used to take place in a common culture.

The political culture has now shifted in ways that pull people apart rather than drawing them together.

Politicians stage rallies that are more about cheering—or disparaging the other side—than thinking and ideas.

Much of our media is divided into conservative and liberal camps, too. Some commentators drive ratings by focusing on the radical extremes, baiting politicians, and distorting viewers' perceptions of the other side, which they position as a dangerous enemy. Social media makes it far easier to spread convincing but fake information without checking first where it came from.

The accuracy of polls continues to weaken as pollsters find it hard to find and model a group of representative voters who will take a moment to honestly answer questions.

The voters in my panel were keenly aware of these forces, but less sure how to address the problem. Any search for common ground has to start by recognizing that modern political culture is very bad at bringing to light what we agree on.

The Pep Rallies
of the President

Trump historically had two channels for whipping up enthusiasm through direct contact with his supporters: Twitter and his rallies. Twitter cut off his account, but the rallies are likely to continue.

Based on my conversations with voters, I think we see the rallies differently depending on how we think about our political positions. For Democrats, the rallies are filled with lies and dog whistles. But for Trump supporters, they're just a chance to participate, firsthand, in the enthusiasm and excitement of a president that understands them. It's not about accuracy. It's about team spirit.

While campaigning for president, and during his presidency, Donald Trump held over three hundred rallies.[1] His supporters, wearing their Trump paraphernalia, camped out in long lines and filled arenas, ready to cheer on their leader. The rallies were oxygen for Trump and, according to some of my voters who attended, a spectacular event for his fans, a place where they made new friends and left full of energy and optimism.

Here's what I wrote about Trump's rallies just a few months after his election as president. It remains an accurate description of what Trump voters feel about the rally culture, even to this day.

Trump and the Rally Culture
April 12, 2017 [2]

According to the April 8 poll from Gallup, 40 percent of Americans approve of the job President Trump is doing.[3] What are those 40 percent thinking? Surely the contradictory messages emerging from the Trump administration, the health care bill's failure, and courts striking down Trump's executive orders should make them think twice. What exactly do they approve of?

Consider Trump's continuing rallies, the ones that prompted Cathleen Decker of the Los Angeles Times to lament his difficulty "leaving behind the ego-stroking mechanics of a campaign for the nitty-gritty of governing."[4]

My conversations with voters over the last 10 months—and specifically with Trump's base—put Trump's rallies in a different light. What if, for our president, campaign mode *is* governing? What if, as Trump insists, the task of "Making America Great Again" is an ongoing campaign?

That would certainly explain a lot.

"My favorite part of Trump's speech to Congress last month," says Tim, 61, a Trump voter from Wisconsin, "was the part about his desire for a renewal of the American spirit." Tim recalls President Johnson imploring citizens to "See America First" in the mid-'60s, prompting Tim's family to pack up the station wagon and head out west. There was a sense of pride in America at the time, and Tim agrees with the president that we need that pride back.

Trump would agree. "Life is a campaign," he told reporters on Air Force One. He didn't seem to think that the rallies should stop once he was in office, and he often talks about the spirit in our country, and even the spirit among his team at the White House.

But what about the lies, say the Clinton voters? The content of a Trump rally is enough to make PolitiFact staffers work deep into the night, to make *Washington Post* reporters document long strings of Four-Pinocchio rulings, a departure from conventional truth that we've never before seen in a chief executive.

But that analysis ignores what Josh Bernoff, author of *Writing Without Bullshit,* calls the rally culture.

Consider it from a fan's viewpoint. At high school pep rallies, we often ignored the weaknesses of our team as we screamed, "Who's gonna win? *WE are!*" Excited about the promise of victory, we would not be happy with a girlfriend who leaned over and announced, "This is a lie, because our team is not that good." Rather than calling her a truth-teller, we'd say she has no school spirit. It's the same at Fenway Park as Red Sox fans sing "Sweet Caroline." It feels good to be part of a rally, and the chants, cheers, and disdain for the other team are all part of the experience.

That's what's happening at a Trump rally. It's people who know they are part of something bigger. Consider the Trump cheers.

"What are we gonna build? *A wall!*"

"Who's going to pay for it? *Mexico!*"

Or:

"What do we think of Obamacare? *It's a disaster!*"

"What do we need to do with it? *Repeal and replace!*"

Or:

"Who had the best victory in the history of the universe? *Trump!*"

Rational arguments and Pinocchios have no place here. If you point out that Mexico is not paying for that wall, you're a buzzkill, and you're going to have to leave, because you're not on our team anymore.

Sometimes it gets meaner.

"What do we think of Hillary Clinton? *LOCK HER UP!*"

You might as well be saying, "Yankees suck!" Because it doesn't matter whether Hillary Clinton belongs in jail—what matters is that we show our opponents that we have power over them.

For these voters, many who have felt forgotten, Trump has given them a voice again. They rallied to Trump's side. And it's going to take a lot more than a few temporary setbacks to get them to leave.

You don't quit on the team when they're down a few runs. And you don't quit on the president who made you feel part of something this powerful, even if the courts are blocking his immigration orders and Congress is failing to pass his favorite bills—because the rally culture is about loyalty and emotion, and not disputed facts or momentary failures.

Trump's combative actions—from lambasting the press as "the enemy" to firing missiles at the airfields of baby-killing Syrian dictators—fit the rally culture perfectly. To keep the rally going, you need enemies, you need emotion, and you need victories. Trump intuitively knows how to supply the drama and the triumphs and to demonize whoever gets in his way. His supporters rally around those feelings, even if, on the face of it, they may seem to be going against their own interests.

Logic and facts make little difference in the face of the rally culture. As long as Trump keeps feeding his fan base, they'll be there for him. It's less about governing, and more about the inspiration. And until Democrats tap into inspiration of their own, Trump's supporters are going to keep cheering.

Understanding Trump Nation

During President Trump's first year, the biggest question I was asked was whether the president's supporters had finally seen the error of their ways. From Muslim bans to the firing of former FBI Director James Comey, they wondered how anyone could continue to endorse a president with such questionable behavior and so few accomplishments.

The voters in my panel told me. In backing Trump, they had found a leader, a set of fellow voters, and a team spirit more inspiring than anything else in politics. And they were going to stick with it.

In order to explain that spirit and enthusiasm that united people on Team Trump, I compared them to how fans of my hometown football team, the New England Patriots, would cheer them on even in the face of cheating accusations. Of course, New England fans didn't think it was a good metaphor.

There's no shortage of personalities in politics—on both sides of the aisle—hoping to replicate Trump's personal appeal and loyalty. But it's not clear whether any of them are up to it—or whether the voters can summon the same enthusiasm for somebody new.

Patriots for Trump

August 1, 2017[5]

"Have they changed their minds yet?"

Over nearly a year, as I have researched voters from all ends of the political spectrum, this is the question I have heard the most from Democrats. Have the Trump voters finally come to their senses? Did that last tweet make them realize how unhinged he is? Are they starting to realize that their lives won't be better with this president?

These are good questions. After all, health care reform has collapsed for now, there is no tax reform yet, White House staff are at each other's throats, and the president is complaining about it all to the Boy Scouts.[6]

Lisa from Virginia is a Clinton voter who agrees: "From where I sit, the American people have to be waking up to Trump. His voters must realize that they have been sold a bill of goods and that the emperor has no clothes."

Ron from Arizona adds, "My friends who voted for Trump are certainly happy about the funding for a wall and the fact that ISIS seems to be vulnerable. I just hope they also see that the swamp is getting thicker and more gooey every day. Give them another year and they will also notice that they have the same old jobs, worse health care, and a president who is just plain clueless about how the government works."

Good luck.

My research shows that although the Trump base has eroded somewhat, at least 25 percent of the country is solidly in his camp and, more important, is not likely to budge.

As Carl from Massachusetts told me, "I don't give a hoot about Donald Trump Jr. and whether he is an idiot. I am not wild about what is going on with the recent staff firings and all of the drama, but I don't care about that much either. I do care about the largest health care fraud bust in history that happened recently. I do care about our economy. I do care that ISIS is almost defeated. I do care about the resolution of this health care bill. I do care about lowering taxes for the middle class. I don't care about an awkward handshake or a bad tweet."

The Trump base believes that he is doing a great job, beleaguered by the mistakes of his staff and constantly taunted by a mainstream media that doesn't want to report on anything that makes the president look successful.

They are solidly on the Trump Team, and that kind of loyalty is rare. Or is it?

In many ways, their passion is like what we see in Patriots fans. Here in New England, the Patriots are beloved: a team that seems to always find a way to win, with a combination of grit, strategy, and talent; a brilliant coach; the most superhuman quarterback in the history of the sport; and a set of values that puts the team first. My friend Ryan, a fan with season tickets nine rows back from the field, loves their work ethic and their commitment to Do Your Job. Ryan and his friends tailgate together, wear the shirts and caps, know every player's stats, and are outrageously loyal. These fans have the Patriots' backs no matter what. In fact, the hell with Spygate, Deflategate, Roger Goodell, and all of the clueless football experts who imply that the Patriots ever even considered cheating. And that includes the media, led by evil ESPN. In fact, the more others bad-mouth the Patriots, the more the fans love their winning team.

Outside of New England, football fans are incredulous. Most feel that we have the worst, most immoral team in the history of any sport and that, on any given day, the Patriots will break rules and ruthlessly cheat their way to victory. Professor David DeSteno of Northeastern University, a social psychologist who has written extensively about the power of teams, explains that people who identify strongly with a particular group tend to look for anything that supports their team and will ignore the bad news.

Like Patriots Nation, Trump Nation has no interest in distractions from people who aren't part of their team. They see critics as jealous losers who like to whine. They explain away the missteps and concentrate on the wins and epic swagger. And just like the Patriots' fan base when, say, the Super Bowl score has you at a 28–3 disadvantage, the worse things get, the more loyal they are, and the louder they cheer. The team needs them, and they need each other.

"How can you not want to be part of Trump Nation?" asks Brad from Ohio. "At the core, we believe in being in charge of your own life. Do you want someone that doesn't know you telling you what to do, how to spend your money, and looking over your shoulder 24/7? No! Do you want to work hard in multiple jobs and then have your money divvied up to the nonworkers? No! There would be no incentive to work then, and the US would become another Third World country."

As Michael from Texas explains, "Trump is doing what he said he was going to do. I don't love the sloppiness, but I give him huge props for his obsession with accountability. He made promises, and he is taking them seriously. Everyone in this country knows what he promised, and now we are watching him trying diligently every day to deliver on those promises—from the wall to repealing Obamacare. You might not like those policies, but those who voted for him do."

He's a different kind of leader, and that's what his voters wanted. Corinne from South Dakota says he's a breath of fresh air, Jerry from Arkansas says Trump is the "action president," and Joe from Nebraska cheers, "The Trump team are novices in the political arena, but remember, that's what we wanted. We didn't want politicians, and so I forgive them their missteps. Drain the sewer!"

From the point of view of voters on the Trump team, their leader deserves respect for trying to keep his promises while he is under siege from a biased press. They know that John Kelly, the White House chief of staff, will find the leakers and that Obamacare is still a disaster.

Many Democrats assume that they can sit by and watch a one-term president who will self-destruct. Sure, it's possible. But it is unlikely that the Trump base will suddenly walk away from the team they love, any more than Patriots fans were willing to jump ship over a few slightly deflated footballs. And the more the base experiences criticism and challenges, the more they will hunker down, put on their red caps, and cheer at the rallies. In fact, if the economy continues to do well, some of those who have recently left The Red Team just might come back.

Clearly, this is our country and not football, but our inability to see both sides of the same coin limits us. What if Democrats worked as hard to understand Trump voters as many people did to understand why some people see a white-and-gold dress and others see a black-and-blue dress in that viral set of photos from last year? Just the same, what if Trump voters did the same in reverse? We could all gain by walking in each other's shoes, by thinking about times when we were so committed to a cause that it seemed to defy logic.

Democrats can come through in the clutch by strengthening their own team and rethinking the priorities of their community. That means more than crying for impeachment or resisting. Instead of feeding on the latest intrigue in the West Wing—a tempting reality show, for sure—a new team needs to form with new leaders and a fresh agenda that inspires more working-class people. The Democrats need a revitalized game plan: their own version of Obamacare 2.0, their own solutions for job growth, a compelling policy for welcoming immigrants into our country, and their own innovative ideas for how the United States can win in the 21st century. That also means finding moderate Republicans to work with and walking away from the partisanship and one-upmanship that belittles our country.

Fake News Distorts
Our Politics

Before Donald Trump ran for president, the term "fake news" referred to false stories—disinformation—planted in social networks to mislead readers. But Trump turned that around, claiming that any story he didn't like in mainstream media like the *New York Times* was "fake news." This naturally increased the degree to which voters became skeptical of everything they read, regardless of the authority of the source. More recently, the Republicans on my panel have denounced companies like Twitter and Facebook for what they perceive to be blatant censoring of conservative voices.

We are also easily duped by stories spreading on social networks. That's what media analyst Josh Bernoff and I wrote about in the piece below.

This problem is deeply entangled with all the others in our politics. Without a diverse media diet, it becomes hard for people to know what to believe. They default to what the most partisan commentators tell them to believe. That encourages more extreme viewpoints and makes it harder for people to listen to and trust each other.

Fake News, Real Consequences

September 13, 2019[7]

"Fake news" is a term, popularized by our own president, that calls into question everything we read and hear from the media. Although it sometimes is used to signify bias, there is a surge in news that is outright fabricated—and it's having an enormous effect on the culture of America. It is surely coming from Russia, but also from right here in our country.

In 2016, Craig Silverman of Buzzfeed compared 20 fake news stories from the presidential election with 20 real news pieces across 19 major media outlets.[8] The fake stories spread faster on Facebook.

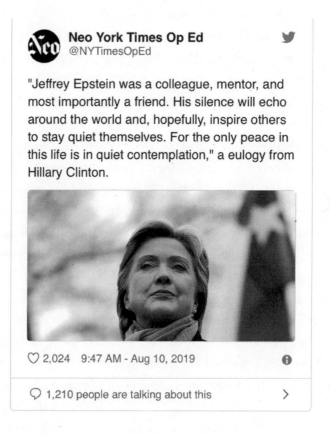

Neo York Times Op Ed
@NYTimesOpEd

"Jeffrey Epstein was a colleague, mentor, and most importantly a friend. His silence will echo around the world and, hopefully, inspire others to stay quiet themselves. For the only peace in this life is in quiet contemplation," a eulogy from Hillary Clinton.

♡ 2,024   9:47 AM - Aug 10, 2019

💬 1,210 people are talking about this

Will the inability to tell real from fake make a difference in who gets elected in 2020?

Most members of Diane Hessan's panel of 500 voters think they know how to test for truth among the vast array of articles, videos, and posts they consume. But when asked to give examples of what influences them, Christina, a well-informed Republican from Pennsylvania, sent this tweet from @NYTimesOpEd, which included a photo of Hillary Clinton:

Christina said this was evidence that "the Democratic Party has lost its way."

Except that it's fake. @NYTimesOpEd is actually the "Neo York Times Op Ed," a parody account. Christina was appalled to learn this. "How would I even know?" she asked. "I mean, it scares me that I didn't figure this out." She said that dozens of her friends were passing the tweet around as if it were legit.

The problem is getting worse, and it's not just Republicans getting fooled. One of our liberal friends furiously defended herself for posting a screen capture of a supposed Trump tweet denigrating community college:[9] "Maybe call it the 13th grade, that's more like it. Community college makes it sound like it's real college and it's not. It's only for dummys." When told it had never actually appeared on Trump's feed,[10] she said "Maybe he deleted it. And anyway, it sounds like the sort of thing he would say."

And, ironically, confusion even happens in reverse: many Americans thought it was fake news—or at least an article from satire site The Onion—that President Trump wanted to host Taliban leaders at Camp David this past week.

Why care about parody accounts and fakery? Democratic Party leader Tom Perez has already fooled a room full of security analysts with a "deepfake" video that appeared to be him but was created synthetically to match someone else's words.[11] It took only one hour—and a budget of zero—for artificial intelligence expert Christopher S. Penn to generate a heap of authentic-seeming fake Trump tweets[12] such as: "I am pleased to announce our new alliance with North Korea. Kim Jong-un and I are great friends. He's doing a fantastic job for his country. I look forward to a future of great cooperation and commerce between the United States and North Korea!" You can go to sites like Zeoob and generate tweets that look completely authentic, blue checkmark and all, such as this fake tweet, which we created in less than a minute:

What is under attack here is nothing less than the idea of objective truth. In the past, we believed that, for the most part, the now much-abused "mainstream media" and other institutions and sources of information—like scientific consensus and the office of the president—stood behind facts you could count on. That trust is eroding. People are substituting their own ideas of the truth, which is whatever reinforces their own prejudices.

This is essential, because once the idea of objective truth is gone, the electorate devolves into a collection of ignorant, easily duped clans.

Here's what to do to make sure this is not you.

First, become familiar with fact-checking sites like Snopes and PolitiFact. Be suspicious of what you read, especially if it reinforces your own ideas too strongly or seems extreme. If fact-checkers say it's fake, read their justification and judge for yourself.

Second, expand your media diet. If you are a fan of Fox News, check out CNN. When it comes to opinion pieces and editorials, balance the *Boston Globe*'s perspective with the *Wall Street Journal*'s. Even if you don't buy the other side's arguments, become familiar with what they are. There is a tradition in American politics of identifying solutions that generate mainstream bipartisan support—like background checks for guns. But you won't even know what the other side is actually saying unless you take a peek.

Third, if it's funny, don't just share it as the truth. In fact, Nieman Lab found that people are often fooled into believing articles on parody sites like The Onion or The Babylon Bee.[13] While parody is protected speech under the First Amendment, you shouldn't confuse it with reality.

Fourth, support legislation to hold social media sites like Facebook and Twitter accountable for spreading lies. These organizations host conspiracy theorists: Mark Zuckerberg has stated that Holocaust deniers aren't violating Facebook policy.[14]

And finally, let's rebuild our children's ability to be skeptical of what they read. They're even more willing than adults to believe what they want to believe online. Our schools should be teaching internet literacy, and as parents, we should, too. Keep your kids safe from lies, just as you'd keep them safe from violence.

We are in a new era, where it seems that all of the information in the world is at our fingertips. It's time to fortify our skills in dealing with the consequences, and to get better at knowing what is real and what is just plain malarkey.

Polling and the Blue Illusion

I n the 2020 election, pollsters predicted a Biden win and a "blue wave" of Democrats elected along with him. In the week before the election, many polls, such as Quinnipiac, NBC News, and YouGov, had Biden winning by double digits,[15] but ultimately Biden received 51.3 percent of the popular vote to Trump's 46.9 percent, and Democrats actually lost seats in the House of Representatives.[16]

As a market researcher for over 20 years, I knew there were substantial challenges inherent in polling—and in predicting outcomes—in our current political climate, and I decided to write about that. We need to admit that polls are part of the political culture now. They can make people feel like part of a movement, or as if their vote won't matter. And when polls can't accurately forecast what will happen, it may cause people to put less stock in them.

The Problem with Polling

November 13, 2020 [17]

"I feel bad because I lied to you," confessed Arlene, an independent voter from Florida whom I had known for two years.

Arlene was part of a group of 500 citizens across the country who had agreed to participate in my project to understand the American voter. When I first interviewed Arlene by phone in 2016, she explained she disliked both Hillary Clinton and Donald Trump, but that she had decided on Clinton after she saw the *Access Hollywood* tape in which Trump spewed lewd comments about women.

In the subsequent two years, Arlene continued to criticize President Trump, although she admitted that, as a business-person, she liked his tax program and his insistence on reducing regulation.

Then, in the fall of 2018, I got a phone call. "I am so sorry, but I just had to tell you, because I worry that I am messing up your data," she said. "I actually voted for Donald Trump in 2016, but if my husband ever finds out, he will kill me—and you can't tell anyone."

Arlene is not alone. People don't always tell the truth to pollsters. Some believe their vote is private and no one else's business, and so they lie to rebel against the intrusion. Others, especially those who planned to vote for Trump this round, worried their answers would be shared and that they could be put into a database of deplorable Americans. Some didn't really know whether they would vote or how they would vote, but they gave the questions their best shot. Or, there is Matt from Massachusetts, who said he told a pollster he would support ranked-choice voting, even though he didn't really understand how it worked. "I just didn't want to sound stupid," he said.

There are many reasons US polling painted an inaccurate picture of a blue wave—with substantial margins—for the November election.

In market research terms, polls can be inaccurate if there are flawed "weights" in the sample, shoddily constructed questionnaire design, or minuscule contact rates.

Weights are used to ensure that the sample has the right mix of people. A pollster might get responses from a sizable sample of 5,000 voters, but if they are all over the age of 60, that skews the results. Although pollsters know this, they are constantly challenged by what to account for in their samples. For instance, in 2016, pollsters determined that they had overweighted for education in their sample. It meant that if only 25 percent of voters in a state had a college degree but 50 percent of respondents had a college degree, the poll's conclusions would not represent the electorate. Getting the weights right is both tricky and important.

Sampling methodology can be as simple as whether you sample any adults or instead base it on citizens who are likely to vote—or whether you survey people in person or online. As for questionnaire design, we know a bad question when we see one, such as the survey question sent to me by a friend last month, "Are you likely to vote and will you support Trump?" The choices were yes and no.

Contact rates are a significant factor. Three years ago, I traveled to the Quinnipiac University Polling Institute, a highly respected polling center. Interviewers worked out of 160 cubicles, making phone calls to voters. As I watched them, I asked myself, "Who answers the phone these days?" and it made me wonder about the challenge of getting anyone to respond; telephone response rates are currently lower than 6 percent. A low response rate doesn't necessarily mean an inaccurate poll in itself, but it does increase the risk of error.

Thus, there are many elements of how pollsters create their models and assumptions that can lead to inaccuracies. When those are coupled with respondents who have no stake in telling the truth, who worry about looking dumb, or who lie just because they resent constant telemarketing interruptions, it's a recipe for polls that don't serve us well. A recent article in the *Globe* reported a new study out of the University of Southern California: that QAnon supporters ruined the data by not participating in polls.[18] The theory was that followers of this conspiracy theory were underweighted in the polls because they distrust institutions and are therefore less likely to respond to a pollster. However, if trust in institutions is the key factor in accurate polling, we should not limit the problem to QAnon.

Fixing this problem requires action on many fronts: larger sample sizes, new methods of getting data that build trust with respondents (such as not having an interviewer with a Boston accent working in Mississippi), and building new models that ensure the weights used for age, education, gender, and political party also include other factors. We need new ways of determining likely voters and better approaches to understanding undecided voters. In my research panel, I got the most trustworthy responses when I asked my voters to predict how others would vote—an indirect approach built on a method called prediction markets.

Here's what we can be sure of: when voters are exhausted, or distrustful of institutions, or concerned about their privacy—or just worried that a friend or family member will discover how they voted—they are not going to put all of that aside for a stranger who calls after dinner. As consumers of polls, we need to remember that polls are not crystal balls. They paint a picture, but they are only as accurate as the willingness of participants to discuss how they will vote—and to tell the truth about it.

Part V

Turmoil in Our Political Parties

Four years of interacting with voters has taught me one clear thing: while people want to believe in and belong to political parties, they're finding it very difficult to do so. Loyalty is fading.

The problem continues on both sides of the aisle.

Among Democrats, the split between moderates and more progressive party members, such as democratic socialists like Bernie Sanders and Alexandria Ocasio-Cortez, continues to make unity challenging. The only thing that everyone could agree on was that they needed to stop Trump. Democratic plans to increase taxes and support people in need met with resistance among the moderate voters in my panel, who are deeply skeptical of any plan to do too much for "free." A compelling example: more than 70 percent of my

Democratic voters are against a plan to eliminate student loan debt; they believe it is unfair to all of the students who have worked hard to pay off their loans already, and that it is an expense that we cannot afford, given competing priorities.

Republicans fare no better. Trump's never-back-down-even-after-you've-apparently-lost campaign left a trail of destruction in its wake, and I don't just mean the broken windows at the Capitol. Traditional Republicans—those who believe that Biden was elected legitimately—are increasingly uncomfortable with the actions taken by those who want to "Stop the Steal." But Trump adherents are fervent, and many elected Republicans are reluctant to break with them. The result is a party fractured in two. In a mirror image of 2016, the only thing they can agree on is that they need to stop Joe Biden, Chuck Schumer, and Nancy Pelosi.

Any party that wants to retain power will have to reach out to the moderates among voters. There are many Democrats who became disillusioned with talk of socialism and Republicans who want nothing further to do with Trumpism. This vast voting bloc is up for grabs and will determine who gets to govern the nation moving forward.

Republicans and Democrats in Disarray

I n 2017, Republicans controlled the presidency and both branches of Congress. Still, other than a tax cut, they were unable to get much done or to find common ground around a set of ideas. And other than resisting Trump, the Democratic Party also seemed to be in disarray, caught between its most progressive members and a more centrist perspective.

What voters wanted then, and still want, is a government that gets things done. What they got was a set of splintered parties, influenced by their most extreme members, unable to get together on much.

My data suggests that there is still a vital center to the American electorate—at least two-thirds of Americans—willing to get behind a coalition of members from both parties to solve the nation's biggest problems.

It's My (Political) Party and I'll Cry If I Want To

December 3, 2017 [1]

"My party is in an absolute shambles," said Arnold from Wisconsin. "They used to represent my beliefs, but they are in disarray and crying out for new leadership."

He's a Republican. But if he were a Democrat, he might well be saying the same thing about the Democrats in Washington. I've finally found an issue everyone agrees on.

In my most recent survey of 400 voters from all ends of the political spectrum, 98 percent agreed that their party is a mess. Voters from both parties use adjectives like "disorganized," "splintered," "weak," and "stumbling." They insist that their parties are letting them down, driven by money and power and extreme voices rather than moral clarity and conviction. Republican voters see a party that has been bought by big business, the NRA, and pharmaceutical companies, whereas Democrats see their party as trying to stand for everything, willing to spend on everything, and also funded by the very wealthy. And then we wonder why voter turnout is so low.

Start with the Republicans. At a time when the party has a majority in the Senate and the House and a leader in the Oval Office, Republican voters are shocked at the lack of much legislative progress in 2017.

Charlene, a Republican from Pennsylvania, said her vote for Trump was taking a position against the Clintons and for change in the Washington power structure. "Drain the Swamp" was more compelling to her than "Make America Great Again," but she now feels that the swamp is getting deeper, due to what she calls the mess within her party. "The Republicans have been corrupted by power-hungry right-wing conservatives, greed, and special interests, and no one knows how to stand up to Trump," she wrote to me. "Where is my party? Where is the party of economic vitality, personal responsibility, and efficient government?"

Enthusiastic Trump supporters are just as unhappy, but for different reasons. "If the Republican Party would support our president, we would be so much better off," said Susan from Ohio. "Instead, they are doing everything they can to get in his way—and we have no breakthroughs in health care or tax reform or infrastructure because our representatives in Congress never did any planning."

This sounds like an opportunity for Democrats, but their voters are just as disappointed. The strategy of "resistance" may have helped turnout in the recent Virginia elections, but most Democrats are crying for a halt to the infighting and a new vision for the future. Whereas the party's most passionate voices are Bernie Sanders and Elizabeth Warren, well over half of the Democratic voters I speak with are interested in less partisanship and much more centrist policies. "When I think of the Democratic Party," said David from Minnesota, "it's like I am watching a divided, confused team playing defense. Perhaps that is needed when Congress and the executive branch are controlled by Republicans, but there is little about that party that makes me want to join it." Added Sheryl from South Carolina, "I feel like the Democrats are still reeling from last year, and have turned into fearmongers badly in need of refocusing."

While the parties are fighting over increasingly extreme positions—and getting so little done—more than two-thirds of voters on either side are begging for moderates to right their respective ships. Some Democrats say they would vote for John McCain over Bernie Sanders. Some Republicans say they would vote for Joe Biden over a candidate supported by Steve Bannon.

It's a tug-of-war, and no matter who pulls hardest, everybody ends up in the mud. This is no way to govern, and it's the reason that voters are so upset.

In a world where technology threatens jobs, North Korea threatens war, and melting ice caps threaten coastlines, the tug-of-war has lost its appeal. Americans are begging their respective parties to wake up: to work together to solve problems, to stop the partisanship and bickering, to talk instead of tweeting, and to stop rigidly supporting positions with no willingness to compromise.

Although nearly half of my group of voters have considered registering as independents, most have ultimately rejected that action because it doesn't solve the core problem, as expressed by Ernie of Indiana, that "at least until now, being moderate is too much about compromise and not enough about innovation."

If the left wants "free health care for all" and the right wants "free health care for none," the compromise, "subsidized health care for many," is not captivating. If the left wants all clean technology and the right wants more coal, it's not as compelling to get a little of each.

This is a time when a majority of voters are willing to move toward the center in order to make progress. Without the intellectual leadership and political will required to reinvent the center, however, all we can do is watch the shambles on both sides, shrug, and resign ourselves to uninspired voters failing to turn out at the polls.

Hysteria among the Democrats

After two years of Donald Trump as president, a major theme from my voter panel was that all they heard from the Democrats was hysteria. What stood out to Americans from both parties were constant insults and profanity in the "resistance"— from Robert De Niro to Samantha Bee to Bill Maher. Surely, they felt, there was a better response to a rude president than to insult him back. Of course, these entertainers don't speak for the Democrats, but they got the ink and the video shares.

In the end, the 2018 election did have elements of a blue wave, shifting control of the House of Representatives back to Democrats. What is difficult to know is to what extent the "twisting and shouting" helped or hindered the outcome. Over the last four years, I have generally found that voters engage with the insults in the short run but are mostly exhausted from the disrespect, the bickering, and the rage. They tell me they want substance, content, and real solutions instead.

Need a Blue Wave? Twisting and Shouting Won't Work

June 20, 2018[2]

"Out of control," "unhinged," and "downright mean." A description of President Trump? Not this time. In my recent voter interviews, these are phrases that voters across the political spectrum have used to describe the Democrats.

"The Democrats have gone from merely disliking Trump to a level of rudeness and resistance unlike anything I have ever seen. It's really cringeworthy," said Fred, a Republican energy-company manager from Akron, Ohio. He added, "My wife and my sons are liberals, and even they are embarrassed at the behavior of the media and Congress."

Katie, a millennial from California and a self-described liberal, said, "I am literally freaking out because liberals are so unwilling to say anything positive about what is going on in our country. We sound biased and hysterical, and it is driving my friends away from the Democratic Party."

Democrats have tried many messages. But only one has stood out with the voters I've interviewed over the last 18 months: "Stop Trump." Is that enough to inspire people to vote against the president? Only about 20 percent of the voters I speak with weekly say so. For the rest, resistance is just not enough to excite them.

Last summer, the Democratic Party rolled out a message called "A Better Deal." Nine out of ten of the voters in my interviews had never heard of it. They hear nothing but negativity, and most believe it has gotten worse recently—that the liberal resistance led by the Democratic National Committee, the media, and Hollywood, has gone from outrage to hysteria, and from logical counterarguments to juvenile behavior and pigheadedness.

Americans were taken aback when Samantha Bee used a vulgar insult to describe Ivanka Trump. The negativity peaked, however, during the weekend of June 10. First, television commentator Bill Maher said he hoped for an economic recession because it was the only way to get rid of Trump. Then, actor Robert De Niro dropped the f-bomb to bash Trump at the Tony Awards. The video of De Niro's attack—and the standing ovation that followed—went viral. The following day, voters in my online community reported that they saw cable news pundits call Trump's meeting with North Korean leader Kim Jong-un "a train wreck in the making," "a naive move," and "merely a reality show with no substance." Even as these two events were happening, billionaire Tom Steyer launched a new series of ads featuring regular Americans who, like Steyer, want Congress to start impeachment proceedings. Although this was an ad, paid for by a private individual, many voters perceived it as yet another part of the negative message.

Democrats report that they have much to be upset about— and some believe that this vigorous, profane resistance will charge up more voters. It doesn't. Instead, it creates backlash, even among moderate voters. And, it emboldens Trump supporters to defend the president, regardless of his actual activities. Said Charlie from Georgia, "The liberals have called us uneducated, but isn't it the mark of intellectual laziness when people cannot find anything positive to say about a summit, anything positive to say about the economy, or the like? The Democrats just sound foolish."

Serena is a Trump voter from New Hampshire, who three months ago told me she was reconsidering whether she made the right choice. "Putin must have pictures," she said in March, "and sometimes I can't believe the sheer stupidity of the president's actions." Today, she has swung back: "Tell a Democrat that the economy is good, and they state that the credit goes to Obama.

Tell a Democrat that Trump's meeting with the North Korean leader is historic, and they will say it was a terrible PR stunt. Tell a Democrat that there are many Trump supporters who are upstanding good Americans, and they will tell you that we are all racist, misogynist bigots. It's ridiculous."

Added Mark, a journalism major at a Boston university, "It pains me to say this, but spin and condescension are the new code of the liberal media."

Democrats—whether on TV, in Congress, or running for office—have a choice.

They can snort that the North Korea summit was a joke—or they can wish Trump well in his historic meeting with Kim Jong-un, even as they express skepticism about how he'll pull off what he has promised.

They can shout that Trump is a pathological narcissist who needs to be impeached—or they can criticize the substance of Trump's actions: his border policies that have resulted in separating children from parents; his contempt for the Paris accords, the Iran Deal, and the G-7 summit; his trade policies that could hurt American companies; his undermining of the Affordable Care Act.

They can wring their hands and hope for a blue wave, or they can create and communicate an array of fresh solutions to our most difficult problems.

From the point of view of voters across the country, shouting and cursing are drowning out any reasoned analysis, turning people off, and sending them back to Trump's corner.

There has never been a time when we more badly need thoughtful, innovative ideas and policies from our leaders and our institutions. We have children at the border who need our collective action, and we have three-fourths of our population living paycheck to paycheck. Giving a standing ovation to De Niro's crude attack does little to address the problems. It may feel great. But it's not going to win elections for the Democrats.

The Need for Excitement and Vision in the Democratic Party

Just before the midterm elections in 2018, Democrats had an image problem. The president, and other Republicans running for office, began to paint Democrats as a group of socialist radicals. Republican voters bought into it. And Democratic voters worried about it.

The primary message Democrats could agree on was "Stop Trump." As it turned out, that was enough for some success. Democrats made a net gain of 41 seats in the House of Representatives, enough to attain a majority. But Republicans unseated four Democratic incumbents in the Senate and increased the size of their Senate majority.

The themes of 2018 also colored the 2020 election. Stop Trump was once again the theme, and the election was at least as much about ejecting the president as it was about electing the Democrat. Republicans, including Trump, hammered hard again on the idea that Democrats were trying to turn America into a country with too much for free, paid for by the taxes of its citizens. And while Democrats attained a 50/50 split and control of the Senate with the help of two surprising elections in Georgia, they lost seats in the House.

Midway through Trump's term, Democratic voters articulated these challenges to me, convinced that their party needed to stand for something more inspirational if it was going to capture their imaginations—and their votes.

Making Waves in the Democratic Party
October 24, 2018[3]

There is little these days that makes Denny more distraught than the Democratic Party. "They are completely out of control," he tells me. "Between the socialists and the rioters, I just wonder what they could possibly be thinking." Denny, a Democrat from Nevada who voted for Hillary Clinton in 2016, is typical of both Democrats and Republicans in the panel of 500 voters I am in touch with weekly.

Last December, when I asked voters about the Democratic Party, most reported that they heard little more than "Stop Trump," a rallying cry that was embraced by the Democratic National Committee when it sent out bumper stickers with that message to millions of supporters.

In my most recent conversations, however, their perception of the Democrats' trademark has morphed into something more troubling.

Let's start with the Republicans. When I ask Republican voters for words to describe the Democratic Party, their response can be summarized as "raging, condescending socialists."

"I actually used to be a Democrat, but then Democrats started screaming and shouting and protesting so much that it alienated me," says José from Texas.

Andrea from Florida blames the Democrats' leaders: "Nancy Pelosi is an angry obstructionist who should be retired." Or, says Nick from Boston, "I see a lot of leaders promulgating a sickening sense of holier-than-thou self-righteousness." "And on top of that," says Lettie from Arizona, "they want to take my hard-earned money and give it all away: free college, free health care, free child care, and guaranteed wages. It scares me."

While Republicans are seeing an intolerant Democratic Party, many Democratic voters share similar perceptions.

"I am concerned about the reputation of my party," says Shandra from New Hampshire. "Who are all of these socialists? And why are we so uncivilized?" Adds Steven from Connecticut, "We are supposed to be the party with the big tent that cares about diversity—and we are on the warpath against at least one third of our citizens. We are in our own way."

Democrats tell me they cringe when they hear Hillary Clinton say that her husband's affair with Monica Lewinsky was "not an abuse of power," when Senator Dianne Feinstein says she would reopen the Kavanaugh investigation, or when former attorney general Eric Holder says, "When they go low, we kick them." They lament these positions because they reinforce the image that Trump has bestowed upon the Democrats: that the party has become "too extreme and too dangerous to be trusted with power" or that "Democrats produce mobs, Republicans produce jobs." When the Democrats lack a clear message, President Trump's rhetoric fills this vacuum with his own caricature, and voters from both sides of the aisle are paying attention.

Certainly in deep-blue districts, it pays for a candidate to be mad as a hornet, but recent studies conclude that this resonates with only about 8 percent of Americans.[4] At a local level, there are Democrats who are rejecting the hysteria, focused on describing a better future for the country. My voters suggested several models, such as Florida gubernatorial candidate Andrew Gillum, whose campaign themes focus on families, faith, and hard work.[5] Instead of proposing a broader array of social programs, Gillum is appealing to the mainstream: "If you work 40 hours a week," he says, "you should be able to make ends meet without having to work two or three jobs."

Massachusetts voters admire how Representative Seth Moulton is staying out of the fray, focused on helping veterans who are running for Congress—or how Beto O'Rourke of Texas reaches out to people who disagree with him. As a group, the Democratic candidates who are military veterans—such as MJ Hegar of Texas, Elaine Luria of Virginia, Ken Harbaugh of Ohio, and Chrissy Houlahan of Pennsylvania—are sending an inspirational message to their constituents about commitment to country, courage, and the fight to give opportunity to all. When Patricia, a Democrat from North Carolina, talks about her support for veteran Dan McCready's campaign for Congress, she tells me, "I don't care about a blue wave as much as a red, white, and blue wave."

The problem is that these Democrats who are taking the high ground are not breaking through enough to influence the overall perception of their party. Blame Fox News, blame social media for putting us into echo chambers that reinforce narrow viewpoints, blame Russian bots, but the Democrats have precious little time to adjust. While it is helpful for former president Barack Obama to say, "I have one thing to say: vote," it's insufficient in countering the message from the right, because it doesn't remind people why they should go to the polls.

What would inspire more voters to vote blue? They would respond to a narrative about rebuilding America for all citizens:

strengthen the middle class, get the deficit under control, rebuild our infrastructure, train the workforce for the future, and restore faith in government—rather than blame, outrage, and resistance.

It also wouldn't hurt if the more controversial past leaders of the party could step out of the limelight for a moment. For instance, given that the Kavanaugh hearings reminded voters about Bill Clinton's history as an accused sexual assaulter, this might not have been the best time for the Clintons to announce their 13-city speaking tour.

The Democrats could very well win the House of Representatives with a message of "Vote for us; we're not corrupt liars like Trump." But there's no certainty that they can govern—or win the presidency in 2020—on a platform that everything's going to be free and the other guys are awful bigots. America is divided. Unless the Democrats can communicate an uplifting image for the nation, it will stay divided, and voters will lose faith in both parties—leaving only the biggest, baddest personalities with any appeal. And we've already seen where that leaves us.

Language Matters: The Case of Radical Socialism

I f I had to pick one reason that Donald Trump did better than expected in the 2020 election, it would be his constant use of two words in the eighteen months before his election: radical socialists.

Democrats brushed this off as one more lie from Trump, as people googled "socialism" and rejected the term. Again and again, the president warned that a Democrat in the White House meant taking everyone's hard-earned tax dollars and using them to give citizens a ridiculous bundle of free services, whether they deserved them or not.

At a speech in Pennsylvania in August of 2020, Biden asked voters, "Do I look to you like a radical socialist?" By then, the response from about half of the Republicans in my panel was yes. The other half thought Biden was too weak not to have his agenda hijacked by the radical wing of his party. Ultimately, many voters told me they were going to vote for someone they disliked because Trump would at least preserve their capitalist system.

Addressing this socialist brand, and its implications for their party, will continue to be a major predicament for the Democrats.

Trump or a Radical Socialist in 2020? Take Your Pick

March 13, 2019[6]

This should be the best time in recent history for the Democratic Party. We have a president who, according to the *Washington Post*, will soon have made 10,000 false claims since he was elected. President Trump's former lawyer, Michael Cohen, just testified that Trump is a racist, a con man, and a cheat. The highly touted talks with North Korea failed. And the federal deficit is up 77 percent as revenues from taxes decline and government spending increases.

"This is our moment," says Angela, a Democrat from Arizona. "The other side is reeling. All we need is to make progress on the issues of the day and to find a terrific candidate for president who can bring us together."

Instead, according to my panel of 500 voters, the party is experiencing an identity crisis of the first order.

"I am so over Trump," says Jeff, an independent from Massachusetts. "But what is the alternative? A party whose stars are a shoot-from-the-hip left-wing extremist and a congresswoman from Minnesota who tweets about the evil-doings of Israel? And a bunch of senior leaders who support them? Virginia state leadership that has demonstrated racism and sexual assault [but] who are still in office because they are not a hot story anymore? And socialism as the new platform?"

Among the 240 Democrats in my panel, over two-thirds agree with Jeff that the party is in crisis. "What are we doing?"

asks Mitchell from Nebraska. "This should be a slam dunk—and instead we can't get out of our own way. We are the party of radicals, socialists, freeloaders, man-haters, and anti-Semites, and I am just praying that we will get our collective act together."

The burgeoning crop of candidates doesn't make voters feel better. When asked whether they see people they would be excited to support among the group, only 28 percent of Democrats answered yes. Says Tim from Colorado, "I mean, even [former Colorado Governor John] Hickenlooper, who is moderate and sane, was barely willing to say he is a capitalist on TV this week. Have we gone mad?"

Jocelyn from New York, a liberal Democrat, sums up the general sentiment: "Unless the Democrats can pull themselves together and come up with a strong, compelling, sane, and electable candidate, we're doomed to—ugh, I can't even bring myself to write it—four more years of Donald Trump."

Most voters I interviewed are not inspired by what come across, variously, as wishy-washy values, an obsession with investigations, and a radical platform—even at a time when the president is stumbling. The Mueller report could change everything—or not. Joe Biden could bring us together—or not. My panel, which reflects the 2016 electorate, might have left out a new crop of Americans who didn't vote in the past but who would turn out for a super-progressive liberal—or not.

It's urgent for the Democratic Party to do some soul-searching. As many candidates line up to propose what seems like free everything for everyone, financed by the rich, they need to ask whether this is the best way to accomplish the party's objectives. Across our country, there is an enormous desire for us to come together as Americans and to make government truly effective. And there is so much common ground on policy: most Americans are for reasonable gun control regulation, for lowering the age at which people can qualify for Medicare, for investing in badly needed infrastructure, for overhauling our criminal justice system, for combatting racism, and for creating a path to citizenship for the so-called Dreamers.

Instead, at least in terms of the optics, voters see a party that is mostly focused on investigating the president. Or, when the Democrats propose legislation, voters see it as too radical. Case in point: the Green New Deal, which includes, on top of climate-change legislation, everything from "repairing historic oppression of vulnerable communities" to guaranteed economic security.

It's almost spring—and much can happen in the next several months. At this point, however, well over half the voters I speak with are concerned that their choice in 2020 will narrow down to a president who acts like a thug and a Democratic contender who is a radical socialist. As the pendulum swings back and forth from far right to far left, it is not too late for something in between that has the potential to bring us together, to give us better choices, and to bring both realism and integrity back to Washington.

Help Wanted:
Better Political Leaders

I n early 2020, after a chaotic and conflicting set of results in the 2020 Iowa Democratic caucuses,[7] the first contest leading up to the 2020 presidential nomination, the Democratic Party still appeared to be in disarray. My voters were not sure what the party stood for, and they were frustrated with the cacophony from so many candidates and messages. Following on the heels of a confusing and ultimately failed attempt to impeach and remove the president, you had to wonder if the Democrats could get their act together.

Of course, no one in February could have seen that the true chaos on the horizon was from what would soon become a raging pandemic, one that got worse over the year despite denials and blame-shifting by the Trump administration. The result was a complete reversal of the Democrats' fortunes and a victory in November.

There are still many conflicting voices in the Democratic Party. And, deprived of a hated opponent, intraparty unity is unlikely. The task is to focus on priorities and to move forward with competence while they still control a majority of both houses of Congress.

Fear and Loathing in the Democratic Party

February 6, 2020 [8]

President Trump has been criticized for running an undisciplined, chaotic administration.[9] But in the last few months, Americans believe the Democrats have been giving him a run for his money. Among the 500 voters I have been in conversation with since Trump took office, the Republicans have certainly noticed the disorder—but now the Democrats are cringing, too, and they are looking urgently for a turnaround.

Start with the chaos that emerged from a failed app that was supposed to collate results in the Iowa caucuses. The Republican National Committee was quick to send a message that if the Democrats can't run a caucus, then they certainly cannot run the United States.[10] As Democratic voter Al from California said, "All of us in tech understand how to test apps. I mean, you have everyone download it a month early, and you do several test runs, and you work out the bugs. How can this even have happened?"

This debacle followed what many perceived to be a misdirected and poorly run impeachment process. Democratic voters are flummoxed that among a range of potentially impeachable offenses by the president (emoluments, obstruction of justice from the Mueller report, and so on), leaders decided to go for broke on an issue related to Ukraine, which, for many Americans, seemed obscure and difficult to fully understand.

Some Democrats found it mystifying that Speaker Nancy Pelosi rushed the impeachment process through the House, then refused to pass the articles on to the Senate for three weeks. And fewer than 10 percent reported that they watched the Senate trial, with most others saying it was either "boring" or a foregone conclusion. "Why read the book if you already know the ending?"

asked Terrence from New York. Jeremy from Massachusetts found the whole impeachment process upsetting: "Literally every branch of government conspired to prevent me from knowing the truth. The White House obstructed. The House rushed their investigation, while the Senate did not conduct what could traditionally be characterized as a trial."

Impeachment aside, the electoral process looks fragmented and confusing. "This is the most important presidential race I have ever witnessed and the Dems' start feels pretty weak, I am sorry to say," said Nancy from Connecticut. Layer on top of that a set of debate rules that have shifted inexplicably, with a decision by the Democratic National Committee to change debate criteria and allow former New York mayor Michael Bloomberg to participate in the debate—even when they would not do this for former candidates Cory Booker and Julián Castro. #TomPerezResign, referencing the chair of the Democratic National Committee, is justifiably trending on Twitter.

It all adds up to a sense of frustration about whether Democrats can make sense of anything in a rough-and-tumble election season. Said Lynnie from North Carolina, "The GOP can speak with one voice, and so far, the Dems are speaking in many voices. This takes away from the voters' focus. So the GOP comes across as having it all together, while the Democrats come across as scattered." Added Tom, also from North Carolina, "When I really let my guard down, I am concerned for the organization of the Democrats. They don't seem nearly as hungry and focused as the Republicans."

Voters worry about the perception that all the Democrats care about is impeachment and investigations, when they should be laser focused on health care, immigration, infrastructure, and the opioid crisis.

The combination of Democratic disarray and Trumpian chaos has created the one perspective that so many on both sides of the aisle can share: nobody is steering the ship particularly well. As Jeremy put it, "As a country, we desperately need better political leaders." And it's only February. We're nine months, 49 state contests, and a bruising election season away from determining who the next president will be. Whether it's Trump or a Democrat, they'll be stuck with an electorate that's restless and angry about the tumultuous state of government. That—more than any particular issue—may be the biggest challenge the country faces if it ever hopes to settle down and do the work of the people, by the people, and for the people.

The Schism in the Republican Party

Written for this book in February 2021.

Allison, a senior at a Big Ten university, grew up in a staunch Republican family. Her father worked in the coal mines, as did most of her relatives, and she learned early in life that fossil fuels were a critical part of America's foundation, that climate change was unfortunate but not man made, that regulation was an attack against freedom, and that China is "out to get us." "I also loved Republican culture," she told me. "In the South, we would go to church on Sundays and drink sweet tea, and I thought that the Republicans wore the snazzy suits and the women had perfect hair. I wanted to be like them."

I have heard hundreds of stories like this from my Republican voters: that being a Republican was something wired into their personal evolution and experience. "My family was Republican and I was taught that it meant that we believed in taking personal responsibility for our lives—that no one was going to help us succeed," said

Greg from Nevada. "It was about small government and low taxes and the American Dream."

Both Allison and Greg left the Republican Party in January of 2021, in the aftermath of the attacks on the Capitol.

Stories of Americans leaving their political party are not new. According to a Gallup Poll conducted in January of 2021, 50 percent of Americans are now independents, 25 percent are Democrats, and 25 percent are registered Republican.[11] I have documented troubles in the Democratic Party in the past (see the chapter titled "The Need for Excitement and Vision in the Democratic Party"), but now there is clearly also strife in the GOP.

The most pronounced tension is between the pro-Trump faction and those they call the RINOs—Republicans in name only—with the implication that they are insufficiently conservative and loyal to have an R on their name plates. Trump supporters, such as Senators Josh Hawley of Missouri and Ted Cruz of Texas, insist that President Trump was an enormously successful leader who was persecuted continuously by the Democrats, who ultimately stole the election from him. The anti-Trump Republicans, such as Congresswoman Liz Cheney of Wyoming and Senator Mitt Romney of Utah, tend to be traditional Republicans in the Ronald Reagan and George H. W. Bush mold, with a desire to move away from the troubling values of the Trump administration and a stated desire to "put country over party."

If my voters are any indication, the party is fractured at the moment, with slightly more Republican voters interested in moving beyond the Trump era, back to a party of conservative values, accompanied by strong morals and increased accountability. Those voters are like Mike from Louisiana, who believes "my party has gone off the deep end," and Robyn from Maryland, who insists that "Trump was less a Republican and more a loose cannon who hijacked the party."

There are few indications of how Republicans could resolve these conflicts.

With increasing numbers of defectors and a growing bloc of independents who are unhappy with both political parties, it's clear that the Republican Party needs to figure out what it stands for. A third party is one possibility, but the investment required to mirror the kind of infrastructure—funding, databases, and staff, for example—makes that a daunting task and thus an unlikely outcome. More likely is that the party goes one way or the other: either pro-Trump Republicans try to purge the party of those they see as disloyal, or the anti-Trump Republicans attempt to purge their party of Trumpism, bringing voters like Allison and Greg back into the fold.

Based on what I hear from voters, there are a few Republican leaders who could bridge the divide, such as Nikki Haley, who is popular among almost everyone in the party, and who is seen as a future presidential candidate. The ultimate outcome might rest with the media, which is could split along pro-Trump and anti-Trump lines, with Newsmax, OAN, and maybe even Trump TV on one side and Fox News on the other. That split would deepen the current divide among Republicans, increase the number of registered independents, and make it difficult to return to the days of snazzy suits and perfect hair.

Part VI

A Human View of Voting Blocs

As I attempted to segment the voters in my panel, I learned that the way pollsters and political strategists think is pretty far from the way voters do. No one wants to be put in a pigeonhole.

The conservative women in my panel were committed to their issues and ideas, not to some conventional idea of what women's issues are.

The young people rejected the characterization that they are just technology obsessed and selfish, and most rejected the term "millennials" because it stereotyped them.

The people who used to be loyal to their political party no longer wanted their leaders making assumptions about their views.

By spending less time talking and more time listening, and by resisting the temptation to place people of the same age or gender or race in the same mold, there is an opportunity for politicians of any stripe to find common ground with voters.

No matter what, today's American electorate is up for grabs.

The Enormous Influence of the Independents

After the election of 2016, it became clear there was a group of voters who were disillusioned with what both Democrats and Republicans had to offer. This was the group I called the New Independents, with a remarkably diverse and nuanced set of viewpoints, but no fixed party affiliation. Some of these voters were actually registered as independents and others told me that they were affiliated with a party, but that they planned to cross party lines often in the future, voting for whomever was the best candidate.

According to the Pew Research Center, the percentage of those registered independent is close to 40 percent,[1] but I found that another 20 percent saw themselves as in this group: a yearning group of voters uninterested in what they perceived as the most extreme positions of the Republican and Democratic Parties. And they are up for grabs because, as I write this, neither the Democrats nor the Republicans have a firm grip on this segment.

Leaders who can find a way to inspire the solid middle of American politics have a potential to turn this voting bloc into a long-lasting stronghold. Biden took hold of them in 2020, but that hold is provisional. They're still waiting.

Meet the New Independents

July 10, 2017[2]

Carolyn is a Republican from Boston. In the past, she had voted enthusiastically for her party's candidates, but she voted for Donald Trump with trepidation. "I didn't like either candidate," she explained, "and so, despite his offensive comments, I went with the anti-politician. The notion of draining the swamp was just really exciting to me, and I saw Hillary Clinton as the president of the swamp." Carolyn also voted for Trump because she wanted lower taxes, less regulation, and a more conservative Supreme Court.

She is still hopeful, but she now believes that Trump turned out to be worse than she had imagined. "Each week, there is a newsworthy event that takes my breath away, and I feel like he is running this country like a dictatorship. I like that the stock market is up, but now I wonder whether I should have voted at all."

Ron is a Democrat from Miami. He voted for Clinton, but is dismayed at how his party has moved so far to the left. "Free college?" he asks. "Do I really want to spend my tax dollars helping middle-class parents, who didn't want to save money like I did, send their children to a college at no charge? And with all of our challenges and the federal debt, can we even afford the programs that are proposed on the Democratic platform?"

Ron hates the content of Trump's tweets, but he is most dismayed by what he believes to be an erosion of our status as a global leader under this president. On the other hand, he adds, "The Democrats are not showing leadership on any front. They have gone limp."

Meet the New Independents: citizens from both parties who are disenchanted with both sides. Although most of the political narrative these days focuses on how divided we are, my data reveal that nearly 60 percent of our country is in this group. They are disgusted with President Trump's braggadocio and volatility, but they see the Democrats as "old and tired faces with old and tired ideas." Says Derek from Philadelphia, "My dismay with the Democratic leadership—an oxymoron—is more than matched by my disdain for the direction of the GOP."

This is important for two reasons. First, these voters are up for grabs. Most say that they would vote outside of their party for leaders who care about country over politics, who have innovative solutions to our problems, and who cater to more than the most powerful and wealthy in America. The Democrats among them applaud Governor John Kasich of Ohio, Senator Susan Collins of Maine, and Senator Lindsey Graham of South Carolina for their willingness to cross party lines. The Republicans among them talk about how they would be open to voting for former vice president Joe Biden if he ran in 2020—or Bill Peduto, the Pittsburgh mayor who transformed that city from a steel town to a vibrant center of "eds and meds."

Second, my math reveals that we have an opportunity to focus, not on how divided we are, but on our common ground. When we focus on the extremes of each party—the voters who believe Trump can do no wrong or the voters who have "Not My President" tattooed on their arms—we can draw the wrong conclusions.

The Trump base among those in my ongoing research group often comment that most Democrats are rioting and protesting and even more, that they do not believe Trump is a legitimate president. That's just not true. Of the 200 Clinton voters in my research, only three are not willing to acknowledge Trump as our president.

Conversely, many progressives perceive that Trump supporters are intellectually lazy, and unwilling to educate themselves about the reality of what is happening in the world. Yet, of the 200 Trump voters in my research, 82 percent read extensively about the issues of the day, and many report flipping back and forth among the various television stations to get a sense of what is real and not. Only 4 percent of those Trump voters support the president unconditionally, whereas most are concerned about his self-absorption, his thin skin, and his reckless tweets.

While we are divided at the edges, many citizens are just plain fed up with the gridlock, the blaming, the resistance, and the notion that, as one voter said, "Neither party represents me or my generation."

There is more nuance than what we often hear from the media. Dan, a Kentucky Republican, wants to repeal Obamacare, but is demanding more gun control. Deb, a Democrat from Oregon, hates the idea of lowering corporate taxes and lifting regulations, but is against sanctuary cities. Mohamad, a Trump voter from North Carolina, supports the immigration ban, but is intensely concerned about the White House's dealings with Russia. Alice from Georgia is concerned about the elimination of environmental regulations and supportive of a significantly higher military budget.

What would an independent movement look like? Rather than seeing us as red and blue, it would focus on the very large swath of the population that is purple. These citizens are hungry for new leaders who operate with the courage of their convictions, who are fed up with insider politics, and who are willing to compromise for a government that works well. A majority of these New Independents want to fix the drawbacks of the Affordable Care Act even as they build on its strengths. Only a few want to eliminate the investment tax for the wealthiest. They want fewer handouts for people who are not willing to work hard. They want progress on infrastructure investment and less talk of a wall at the Mexican border. Some are abortion-rights proponents and some are antiabortion, but most talk about the seriousness of a decision to have an abortion, and they see progress in the news that rates of abortion are at a historic low.

It's time to pay more attention to this group. Many of them believe that the 2016 election was about voting for the lesser of two evils, between two candidates who had integrity issues. They now want leaders who are driven by a commitment to helping others rather than a commitment to party and ego. And they will support politicians who, instead of immediately trafficking in blame or criticism, are ready to work to solve our country's problems.

What Women See in Donald Trump

W omen are not a voting bloc.

Yes, women are more likely to vote for a Democrat than a Republican. And based on exit polls in 2020, women voted for Biden over Trump, 57 percent to 42 percent.[3] (Men were more likely to vote for Trump than Biden.)

But from my research with fifty women who voted for Trump, I learned that it would be a mistake to see women as a monolithic group concerned about "women's issues" such as abortion or breaking the glass ceiling.

The piece below received more comments and social media attention than almost anything I have ever written.

About Those "Women for Trump"
January 24, 2020[4]

"It would make me so excited to vote for a woman for president," said Alice from Michigan. "I do think I will see one in my lifetime, and, as the mother of a daughter, it would especially thrill me."

Yet Alice voted for Donald Trump in 2016 and expects to vote for him again in 2020. When I asked her why she didn't vote for Hillary Clinton, she said, "Hillary is an elitist Democrat who doesn't care about women like me." Alice wondered if liberal women would be willing to vote for female candidates like Nikki Haley, Ivanka Trump, or Condoleezza Rice.

What is in the minds of women who support Trump? This is a key question people ask me about the panel of 500 voters with whom I've interacted since 2016. They want to know how any woman can vote for a bully, whether they care that he has been accused of sexual assault by multiple women, how they can support a president who puts children in cages, or why they would support someone who wants to take away the Affordable Care Act, a.k.a. Obamacare. Isn't this a terrible model for their children?

To answer these questions, I took a deep dive with 50 women who support Trump. I found two overarching themes: first, that women valued Trump's policies over anything else, and second, that they saw Trump as a refreshing change from those they perceive to be elitist candidates of either gender who failed to understand and respect the power and determination of conservative women.

Women could be the difference in the presidential election. According to the Pew Research Center, women tend to vote at higher rates than men. And numerous studies of voters in key swing states, like Pennsylvania, Michigan, and Wisconsin, have found that white working-class women could determine the next president.

Policy—especially linked to the economy—matters deeply to women who voted for Trump, and to them it outweighs his coarse behavior. "In spite of all of the resistance, he has accomplished so much that is important to me," said Dianne from New

Hampshire. "Our economy is booming, unemployment is low, homeownership is up, our defenses are being reinforced, ISIS is weakened, and he is getting fairer trade deals." Again and again, women stressed the health of their local economies: building booms, more jobs, and more people out shopping. And they credit the president for their prosperity.

The other big factor for female Trump voters is what they call his "respect" for them, a fundamental belief that Washington is run by people with multiple degrees from elite schools who look down upon them. They dwell on Barack Obama's statement that they are bitter and clinging to their guns and religion and Hillary Clinton's remarks about deplorables. Before Trump, they felt that they had no voice and no power. Said Anna from Iowa, "Donald Trump actually likes and respects people like me. He gets that the average citizen of the USA is not stupid, and the Democrats have not figured that out yet."

These factors outweighed Trump's boorish behavior. "He is not a politician," said Susan from Ohio. "I wouldn't want my daughter to date him, but I wouldn't want her to date Bill Clinton or JFK or any of the other predators who have been in the White House."

Trump also appeals to women who feel that the women's movement has left them behind. Katie from North Carolina described it this way: "You know, not all women are pro-choice, not all women obsess over the glass ceiling, and many women want smaller government and a continued good economy." Added Cynthia from Massachusetts, "The women's movement does not represent me. A Women's March with no conservative women involved? A real women's movement would embrace all of us. It would fight for equal pay, equal opportunity, personal safety, and assistance in raising future generations. But feminists of today detest people like me, so why would I want to support them?" A majority of these Trump supporters feel alienation from liberal women, whom they perceive to be "angry" and "fist clenching."

Some of these women are open to alternatives to Trump—so long as that alternative isn't too radical. Said Chrissy from New Jersey, "I am embarrassed by his tweeting and his behavior, and I also believe that we need someone who is less divisive—but I don't see a choice when the Democrats stand for giving everything away for free."

> *Two stone cold losers from Amazon WP. Almost every story is a made up lie, just like corrupt pol Shifty Schiff, who fraudulently made up my call with Ukraine. Fiction!*
>
> **—Donald J. Trump (@realDonaldTrump)**
> *January 20, 2020*[5]

For every woman like Chrissy, however, there are many others who will support Trump regardless of who runs against him. They sound like Brenda from Pennsylvania. "He is the most transparent president ever, and he follows through on his promises," she said. "He loves and supports his family, and he respects my money, rather than wanting to squander it."

Women who support Trump know what they are looking for, and they believe it's not what the Democratic front-runners are offering. They would advise Democrats to abandon impeachment, censure the president, and focus on how to fix our broken country. They want answers to questions such as: How will you keep our economy booming? How will you continue to keep jobs plentiful? How will you manage our illegal immigration crisis? How will you control the growing costs of health care? How will you give our children better lives? And how will you do this without increasing my taxes?

Many Democrats would probably compare these comments to hearing fingernails on a blackboard, convinced that women who support Trump live in an alternate universe. And most polls find resounding support by women for a Democratic candidate over Trump in November. Thus, one path for Democrats is to give up on these women and focus on a different segment, such as the youth vote. This is certainly what the Trump campaign is banking on, as they invest in Women for Trump events and outreach in battleground states that are likely to be pivotal in the general election.

Is there a way to win the hearts of these women? Unless another candidate comes along who they believe respects them and their pocketbooks, they won't be buying the book *A Very Stable Genius*. Instead, they'll vote to reelect the president.

The Trump Voters Who Switched to Biden

I n May of 2020, of the 220 voters in my panel who had voted for President Trump, 33 had deserted him. Looking back on what they told me, I could see the outlines of the 2020 election forming.

I call these voters "disillusioned" because that's how they sounded. They were initially thrilled with most of Trump's policies. But two things turned them off: his relentlessly bad behavior, revealing what they believed was a seriously flawed character, and his inability to appropriately manage the COVID-19 crisis.

Even so, those Republicans who, in 2020, voted for Biden—or a third party, or stayed home—are not converts. If a candidate comes along that combines Trump-like policies with a presidential bearing and competence, these voters will be drawn back to them.

My impressions of this portion of the electorate highlight its high degree of volatility. Between the extremes, there is a broad group ready to bolt. The question is, who might inspire them next?

Disillusioned Trump Voters—Up for Grabs

May 29, 2020 [6]

"President Trump has completely worn me down." That's what Fred, a Republican from New Mexico, told me. "I've been pretty darned patient, but his propensity to deny what is glaringly real and his propensity to outright lie—I mean, good golly, Molly." Fred voted for Trump in 2016, and he is one of 33 voters from my panel of 500 who gave Trump the thumbs up initially but who is now repulsed by his leadership. To understand the electoral plans of this voting bloc, I interviewed them in depth.

In 2016, these voters opted for Trump partially as a vote against Democratic nominee Hillary Clinton, whom they perceived to be untrustworthy and condescending. Even more, they took a flier on Trump because they liked his economic policies, his beliefs about smaller government, and his plans to shake up the Washington bureaucracy. Sue, who lives in Washington, DC, liked that "he was willing to forgo political correctness and connect directly with issues that I felt were important and needed airing," such as free enterprise and the need to correct what she calls "our entitlement society." Today, these voters defend Trump's progress on the economy, his actions to eliminate overregulation, his stance on China, and his efforts to halt illegal immigration.

But they were expecting Trump to mature in the job, to mellow over time. Instead, they perceive President Trump to be the same as candidate Trump—even three and a half years later.

Said Andrew from Wisconsin, "I am surprised at the lack of character growth over his presidency. I really thought he was going to grow into the role more." These voters expected that Trump's divisiveness and "immaturity" would subside over time. Robert from Massachusetts noted, "There was never the presidential pivot. He remained a petty, name-calling bully not fit for the leader of the free world."

Across the board, these voters are less averse to Trump's policies than they are to his comportment. They describe him as "childish," "narcissistic," "stubborn," "insecure," "bombastic," and "a moron." Added Chris from New Jersey, "He is so crass and really needs to tone it down. Why can't he focus on bringing our nation together?"

> *When will they open a Cold Case on the Psycho Joe Scarborough matter in Florida. Did he get away with murder? Some people think so. Why did he leave Congress so quietly and quickly? Isn't it obvious? What's happening now? A total nut job!*
>
> **—Donald J. Trump (@realDonaldTrump)**
> *May 12, 2020*[7]

The predominant policy position that disappoints this group is Trump's extreme stance on the environment. As Chris said, "I do believe in global warming, and he not only denies climate change, but he has gutted agencies and policies that would have helped our planet." Otherwise, for these voters, their dissatisfaction is all about Trump's personality.

The key question for the election, of course, is: Are Trump's shortcomings severe enough to get them to vote for the presumptive Democratic nominee Joe Biden? Most are still wavering.

Of the 33 participants, five plan to vote for Biden, seven will still vote for Trump, eight will stay home rather than vote, and the remainder are undecided. As they were in 2016, these voters tend to be unhappy with both candidates and expect to go into the voting booth holding their noses. As Tim from Colorado asked,

"Are these really the best two people we can find in a country of 330 million? We have a duty to vote, but we also have a duty to put decent candidates up to vote for—and both parties have fallen short."

Many express concerns about Biden's mental acuity and his ability to bring fresh energy to our country. Adam, a New York voter, suggested that Biden's current silence and gaffes must be replaced with something more inspiring: "Biden needs to come out and start demonstrating he can and will take over and make our future better than anyone else, to show us that he is a force to be reckoned with." Biden supporters might defend their candidate and cite his media presence of late, but these disaffected Trump voters haven't seen much that captures their imagination.

Disillusioned Trump voters have advice for Biden. Chuck from Oregon, who thinks Trump should "stop getting up in front of the microphone and stop tweeting," said Biden "should get in front of a microphone and start tweeting." As for Biden's vice-presidential nominee, most say it will make a difference only if Biden chooses a "radical" like Senator Elizabeth Warren of Massachusetts or Senator Kamala Harris of California, in which case they are less inclined to vote for him. Predictably, for this group of former Trump voters, Senator Amy Klobuchar of Minnesota would be their preferred pick—or even someone from the other party, like former secretary of state Condoleezza Rice or Trump's former ambassador to the United Nations, Nikki Haley, who they believe would put teeth into Biden's promise to unite the United States.

Trump's weak coronavirus pandemic performance could still sink him with these voters. They don't fault the president for a slow start, citing the uncertain and unprecedented situation—but they do condemn his leadership during this crisis. "Pretending that it's not bad or that it's over, and saying that we will defeat

COVID by Easter, was just ridiculous," said Michelle, a North Carolina resident. Many others denounced Trump's inability to "get out of the way," and his failure to model the very policies our government is advocating. "For God's sake, wear the damned face mask," pleaded Christina from Pennsylvania.

We already know that voter enthusiasm will be a critical factor in November. Yet with an ineffective White House, high unemployment, politicians who mostly blame one another, and a pandemic that seems to have no end, these former Trump supporters are both exhausted and demoralized. Initially engaged and hopeful about the future, they now seem resigned and skeptical about the federal government's ability to improve our lives. Many wonder if their votes will really matter. At the moment, this segment of disaffected Trump voters is small, but in light of the president's shaky coronavirus performance, it's likely to get larger in the next several months.

Although voters determined to vote for Trump probably won't change their minds, there remains an important group who are undecided or who are currently sitting on the sidelines. There is still time for an inspiring, clear-minded Joe Biden to energize them.

Being Black
in America

Many of the problems that keep Americans from finding common ground boil down to an inability to understand someone else's perspective.

There is no more visible demonstration of this than the experience of being Black in America.

I heard this often from the forty Black voters in my panel. Black Americans overwhelmingly voted for Hillary Clinton in 2016, demonstrating that Donald Trump did not capture the imagination of everyone facing economic anxiety. In general, I found Black voters to be more likely to be Democrats, more likely to be politically moderate, more likely to talk about the importance of compassion, and very aware—and proud—of their increasing influence in national elections. To a person, they were supportive of the Black Lives Matter movement, but not always of the BLM organization, which some told me was too radical, too anti-Semitic, or just too controversial. Across the board, they remarked that white Americans, including their friends, were not able to comprehend what it is like to walk in their shoes.

I wrote this column as an emotional reaction to what happened in Central Park in May of 2020. A Black man named Christian Cooper, a birdwatcher, approached a white woman with a dog and told her the dog was required to be on a leash according to park rules. She responded by calling 9-1-1 and reporting that an African American man was threatening her life.

This is a very different kind of piece for me, since it is based so heavily in my own experiences and those of my friends. But every Black person in America knows what it is like to have people presume they are out to cause trouble, merely because of how they appear.

It's Past Time for White People to Step Up

June 19, 2020[8]

I am sitting in the passenger seat of my friend Barry's car in Norristown, Pennsylvania, after a high school football game. A policeman has pulled us over and motions for me to roll down my window. I am petrified.

"Are you okay, miss?" the policeman asks.

"Yes, I am fine," I reply.

He pauses, and then says, "Okay, just checking."

On the driver's side, the policeman's partner has asked Barry to exit the car and show his driver's license. Eventually, they allow Barry to get back into the car.

We look at each other. Did they think I was being kidnapped? I'm shaken.

Did I mention that Barry is Black?

When I tell this story to my Black friends, they're not shocked. "Happens all the time," they say.

What "happens all the time" to Black Americans must be front and center as we confront systemic racism in our country.

The conversation lately is centered on police violence. After the police killing of George Floyd, I asked my panel of 500 voters if police are more likely to use excessive force against Blacks than others. Sixty percent responded true, 35 percent said it was false, and 5 percent didn't know. When asked if Black Lives Matter, their results were similar. All who disagreed with the statement were white, and 93 percent of them voted for President Trump in 2016.

Do Black people face daily and pervasive prejudice from the police and others or not?

Instead of asking the forty-eight Black voters on my panel, I reached out to the upper echelons: to a few dozen Black colleagues who have been successful despite it all: a hedge fund manager, a McKinsey consultant, a doctor, a former Fortune 500 CEO, a real estate developer, an advertising executive, and so on. Although on the surface these individuals are at the top of their respective professions, their experiences are heartbreaking. Imagine being in their shoes.

- You go to a boarding school. Your roommate's family sees you and then requests a new room assignment for their daughter.

- You change the first name on your resume, because the name you were born with is likely to create prejudice and cost you the interview.

- You enter a sauna at your health club. Another patron asks you for more towels.

- When you go shopping, store personnel follow you around to make sure you're not stealing.

- When you walk around in Boston, you wear an Ivy League college shirt to signal that you are not dangerous.

- Your Uber driver pulls up, then speeds away as they see your face.

- You are invited to play at a golf club, then when you arrive, the receptionist makes four phone calls to make sure it's okay to let you in.

- At a networking event, you approach a group of professionals, and one turns to you and asks for another scotch.

- As you head for your first-class airplane seat and put your luggage into the overhead bin, another passenger says, "That bin's for first-class passengers only."

- You're a doctor. Patients in the waiting room see your face, then get up and leave.

- You are pulled over so often in your Mercedes (which you worked hard to earn), on suspicion of stealing it, that you sell it and buy a Toyota.

The list goes on. If this is happening to those at the top, what is happening to the majority of Black people in America?

Every one of my successful Black friends is afraid of the police. They have been stopped dozens of times: in their cars, on the street, in fashionable neighborhoods. They have been stopped for driving one mile over the speed limit, for having a taillight out, for turning without signaling, and for no reason at all.

They worry about whether their husbands will come home alive.

They notice that protesters are more diverse than ever, and that is heartening—although they wonder why it has taken so long for us to wake up.

They believe that what happened to Christian Cooper in Central Park is terrifying because with one phone call, the white woman confronting him could call the police and put his life at risk.

They say that they don't talk about their stories because they have been advised to pick their battles and to keep their heads held high.

Some have cried every day for the last two weeks.

And they are completely exhausted at being warriors for justice.

I thought I understood. I grew up in a steel town in an integrated high school—and I had lots of Black friends. We played at each other's houses and knew each other's families. So I thought I was pretty woke about prejudice and discrimination.

Now I know that I have much work to do, and that we white people need to step up: to confront the notion that addressing racism in our country is not just about reforming police departments, but also about reforming ourselves. We need to get educated about the unequal treatment and humiliation and degradation that Black people have faced for centuries—since 1619—because of the color of their skin, and how racism robs people of their dignity.

We must confront how society works differently for white people. Just because I was in Barry's car doesn't mean that I understand—because I never had to fear for the next time I was driving. When I am stopped by the police for speeding, I worry only that I will get an expensive ticket and my insurance rates will increase: one small example of my white privilege. And for those who respond, "All Lives Matter" when they hear "Black Lives Matter," that is, as my friend Noam says, like going to a pancreatic cancer walk with a sign that says, "All Cancers Matter."

Racial justice is everybody's problem, and we are having important conversations about it. Let's not go back. Let's decide that if we care about our high ideals, we will act, and unleash all the potential that lays dormant in our world. When Martin Luther King Jr. was assassinated, we thought things would change; when Rodney King was savagely beaten by the Los Angeles police, we thought things would change. But they didn't. Instead of making 2020 the year that we were crippled by the coronavirus, let's make it the year we all finally committed to ensuring that all Americans have the right to life, liberty, and the pursuit of happiness.

The Potential Power
of Young Voters

On the eve of the 2020 election, I wrote, "If voters under 35 came out at the same rate as those over 60, they could decide the election." That was certainly the case. More than 52 percent of eligible voters under 30 voted, as compared to 42 to 44 percent in 2016.[9]

Young voters who in the past might have said, "It's too much hassle, they're both the same" turned out, because the candidates were very clearly *not* both the same. Biden, the oldest president ever elected, has these enthusiastic young voters to thank, at least in part, for his election. According to research done at Tufts University, 61 percent of young voters turned out for Biden, compared to 36 percent for Trump.[10]

The question now is what happens to their issues: gun control, youth unemployment, and global climate change, for example. These voters tell me they are looking to Democratic Congresswoman Alexandria Ocasio-Cortez of New York or Republican Congressman Madison Cawthorn of North Carolina to represent them in the future. Political leaders will have to find ways to keep these voters engaged, or they'll see youth turnouts drop back to historically low levels.

Young People, Get Out Your Vote
October 16, 2020 [11]

Hugh, an independent voter in Massachusetts, is planning to vote for President Trump in the November election. As one of 500 voters on my panel, he has been in constant contact with me over the last four years. He's educated, politically engaged, and passionate about our country. He's also a grandfather of 22 children, 14 of whom are of voting age. Of those 14, only three plan to vote.

This is hardly an aberration. In the 2016 presidential election, nearly three times as many older people (ages 60+) voted as younger people (18-29).[12] In this year's presidential primaries, turnout among eligible youth voters was also low. Participation rates by voters under age 30 were less than 20 percent in each of the 14 states that held primaries on Super Tuesday.[13]

Increasing turnout among younger voters should matter to any American interested in determining the course of our country. The 104 Democratic and Republican voters under age 30 on my panel differ based on their respective parties; Republicans tend to be antiabortion, pro-business, and anti-immigration, whereas Democrats are the opposite. However, there is also common ground: younger voters are more likely to be passionate about climate-change legislation and gun control, which they see as defining issues for their generation.

Younger voters have various reasons for not getting their ballots in. Some say neither candidate inspires them. Those from deep-red or deep-blue states believe their one vote won't matter.

Jeff, 28, from Connecticut, told me he is just too busy. "I'm in the middle of launching a startup and it's 24/7," he said. "There is no time for me to make voting a priority."

Caroline, 27, from New York, plans to vote, but she recounts a cumbersome process with "all the checking online (on very old, unclear websites), to find out if I was registered." She was required to print out her credentials—when few in her generation own a printer—locate an envelope, and find a car to drive to City Hall. "Millennials are used to working at warp speed, and voting takes a significant amount of time and effort," she explained. She described voting as "tedious, bureaucratic, and outdated," with multiple temptations for young people to drop off at any step along the way.

Jose, 24, from Texas, feels that government doesn't work for him. His student loans weigh on him, and he still lives with his parents because he can't afford a place of his own. "Neither of the old white guys seems to have a solution for me," he said.

Some young people are excited to cast their ballots, like Nick, a student at Boston University, who told me that "to be derelict in my duty to partake in crafting the future of our country is to turn my back on that country itself." However, even those who are committed to voting acknowledge that many of their friends might stay home.

Still, youth turnout could be higher in November than in the past. According to Tisch College at Tufts University, voter registration among young people is up over the 2016 election, led by increases of more than 25 percent in Georgia, Idaho, Kansas, and New Jersey.[14]

There are numerous strategies for encouraging young people to vote: get-out-the vote campaigns on college campuses, ads on social media, and organizations that are mobilizing young people directly, such as Rock the Vote. Their messages focus on telling young people that they can make a difference, with reminders that our ancestors fought hard for the right to participate in democracy.

One strategy that could also encourage young people—especially Democrats—to vote is reverse psychology. We might share with them the perspective of Keith, a passionate Trump supporter from North Carolina: "I hope they all stay home! Ninety-nine percent have never worked, never paid taxes, think they are ENTITLED to $15 minimum wage, and deserve free everything! Stay home, you basement-dwelling, safe-space loving snowflakes!" (Although Keith's statement isn't accurate—a Harvard Business Review article laid out the case that millennials tend to be workaholics[15]—young voters might be motivated to prove Keith wrong and run to the polls.)

There is a profound opportunity for younger voters to become the most influential voting bloc in November. It starts with their realizing that power is not a chicken/egg proposition.

The presidential candidates are speaking loudly about health care and lower drug prices and less so about student loans because they know that older people vote. Youth voters may be waiting for a candidate who will eliminate their debt, provide affordable housing, and so on, but that won't happen if a candidate will win even if they don't fight for those issues—at least under the current circumstances. On the other hand, no candidate would ever argue successfully to lower Social Security benefits, despite the financial case, because elderly people vote in droves and the candidate would lose in a landslide.

The message to young people must be that voting, with all of its friction and hassle, leads to power and influence—that if voters under 35 came out at the same rate as those over 60, they could decide the election. They would then have the influence they covet, as candidates shift their policies to attract this new and forceful voting bloc.

The dream is this: that when we reflect back on 2020 and speak about the profound shifts in our country, one of those will include an election that all came down to our youth—who finally got it, who came out despite the antiquated systems and competing priorities, and who became the most impactful political force in the history of our nation. Let's all hope they rise to the occasion.

Part VII

A Path Forward: The Power of Listening

Four years of listening to Americans—without judging—made a powerful change in my perspective on the world. I got to know them. And I began to recognize that, whether or not they agreed with me on this issue or that, this political leader or that one, or even which facts were true and which were not, we were after the same thing. We wanted a nation, a government, and leaders that worked for us and our families.

I also learned a lot about the "polarized" state of America.

It is absolutely true that we have disagreements on some very fundamental issues. It is also true that we have distorted perspectives of each other. We perceive those whose opinions diverge from ours as not just different, not just wrong, but deluded and dangerous. And we forget that the deranged radicals in our country are not typical representatives of their political parties.

This is true despite the fact that, as I have shown, there is an awful lot of common ground in what we want for America and even on some of the ways we might get it. There is plenty of room for agreement.

But everything about the way we interact with others now—our red and blue communities, red and blue television networks, red and blue candidates, and red and blue filter bubbles in social media—tends to pull us apart.

How can we connect?

It all starts with making the effort to listen, and with learning better ways to do it.

This may seem like a simplistic solution to a complex problem. Perhaps it is. But let me share what I've seen happen, and perhaps I can convince you of the power of listening.

The Story of Aviva and Doug and Joseph

Joseph Arrambidez is one of the members of my panel of 500 voters, a Hispanic from Texas who voted for Donald Trump in 2016 and 2020. In November of 2020, Joseph agreed to write an opinion piece for the *Boston Globe* about the Republican point of view and why he believed we would not be united as a country.[1] He wrote passionately about our division:

> If I want strong borders for our country, I'm told that I like to separate children from their parents and put them in cages. We hurl insults instead of talking about the common sense of ensuring we have only legal immigration, as many other countries do. If I believe we should lower taxes on those who create jobs so others can have gainful employment, I'm told

the rich are greedy and evil and should pay their fair share, as if they don't already do so.

Aviva Brooks, a Democrat from Brookline, Massachusetts, read Joseph's piece and wrote a letter to the editor expressing her interest in speaking with Joseph.[2] I passed along the contact information, told Joseph to expect an email, and didn't think much of it.

Months later, I learned that Joseph, Aviva, and Aviva's husband, Doug, have been talking over Zoom for months. They didn't have a plan—only a commitment to listen and try to understand each other. "I read that piece and just felt compelled to respond," Aviva told me. "I am one of those people who believes that we have more in common than what separates us, and that we just need to talk."

Joseph agreed to have a conversation. "Aviva said she disagreed with most of what I was saying in my opinion piece, and that she really wanted to understand me," he said. "I decided to speak with her because I wanted to know what it would be like to talk to someone from another part of the country. Texas is close to the border and Massachusetts isn't—and so that probably meant we saw the world differently." Both said that they were nervous before the first call, but that their worries quickly faded once they started talking.

Their first meeting lasted an hour and a half. With no agenda and no plan, they just decided to get to know each other. Although both admitted to being a bit nervous, they found commonality right away. They both loved to cook—BBQ for Joseph and lentils for Aviva. When Joseph talked about his dog, Zeus, Doug recalled that his late uncle had created a wall chart of the Greek gods, and he shared more detail about Zeus, the ruler and protector of all gods.

Since then, they have spoken monthly, sometimes dealing with tough topics such as the presidential election and their views of the Capitol Hill attacks on January 6, 2021. They both told me that the dialogue they are having is an extraordinary learning experience, and that they are opening their minds with each call.

"It's unlike anything you would have ever thought," Joseph said. "Most of what we see and read has so much vitriol to it. So I hardened myself, blocked things out, and put up walls. Talking to someone from what you *think* is the other side of the world gears you up for a fight. But I could tell in our first thirty seconds that it was not like that. I feel like we have been friends for years."

Joseph also talked about how interesting it is to hear another point of view. "Ninety percent of my neighbors are Trumpsters, and we talk about the same things over and over like we are in a clique. With Aviva and Doug, it is a new view into the world." As Aviva wrote in a second letter to the *Globe*, "Neither of us feels the need to walk away a winner."[3]

Aviva added, "What has really worked for us is an agreement that we listen in order to learn rather than listening in order to respond or win an argument. It's about having an open mind and an open heart and finding the humanity in people." She told me that with Joseph, she doesn't feel that she is talking to a "Trumper"—that she is speaking with a human being who, like her, is trying to do the best he can with his life. She said, "I am proud and honored to call Joseph my friend."

Doug, an attorney who specializes in pyramid schemes and scam artists, was naturally skeptical in the beginning. Although he is more of the debater in the family, he wanted to be part of the conversations because the disagreements in our country are so painful. "I have learned that if you want this dialogue to happen, it really does work." Aviva and Joseph give Doug credit for being "the calm in the conversation."

Their friends all know about the conversations. In the beginning, Aviva's friends thought she was incredibly brave, and unlikely to be successful, given their own experiences disagreeing with their relatives.

Joseph's friends had similar reactions. One remarked, "Man, that's a good idea, but I don't have the stones to do it. Aren't you worried you will get eaten alive?" Now, however, their friends and family enjoy getting updates on the latest conversation, and they say they feel excited and inspired.

Their advice for others? It's what Aviva wrote in her second letter to the *Globe*: "As the old commercial says: Try it, you'll like it. Reach out to someone who doesn't look or think like you, or who doesn't believe or vote as you do. Or accept such an invitation, including those invitations dressed as disagreement. Stay connected. Weed through your differences and celebrate your commonalities. Know that at least one commonality binds us: that together we can begin this long road toward unity, even if with one small step."[4]

Listening Without Lecturing: The Magic of Conversations

The Greek philosopher Epictetus gets credit for the saying "We have two ears and one mouth so that we can listen twice as much as we speak." Maybe your mom said the same thing. Listening hard is the most important act we can engage in if we want to show someone respect and empathy—and if we want to have any chance of breaking down the barriers and assumptions that divide us.

We already know that, right? And yet, for some reason, when someone is in a difficult situation, we listen a bit, but many times we unconsciously decide we are so smart that we should try to solve their problem. We offer well-meaning advice, send newspaper articles, and tell stories of the people we know who have been in the same predicament. We talk instead of working on hearing the other person.

When tensions are high, it gets worse. We have an argument with someone, and our most frequent response is, "Oh yeah? Well, let me list all of the things you have done wrong." It's rare that we say,

"I know you are mad at me. Help me understand what's going on from your point of view." We just aren't in the mood to do that—even though when we listen hard, the other person is much more willing to listen to *our* point of view.

When I worked on research for the Clinton campaign in 2016, I often would interview Americans who loved candidate Trump, and I knew that if I had any chance of changing their minds, it would never happen if I just listed all of Hillary Clinton's assets and all of the awful things Trump had done. Instead, I was more successful when I listened hard enough to understand first what was behind their enthusiasm.

To do this, we don't need to be professional psychologists. We can try it with our friends, our children, and our partners. Instead of giving advice or convincing them of our point of view by showering them with evidence, we can listen and try to understand. The more people talk, the more we learn, and the better they feel.

Listening Hard

What does it mean to listen hard? Let's say you are going to talk about gun control with someone you know feels differently than you do. The best structure is usually to start with one person listening to the other until you really understand their point of view; when you finish that task, switch roles. Joseph Durzo, a former coworker of mine who runs DDG Management Advisors, unpacked listening in a project for The Forum Corporation in the 1980s and created what is still the best set of guidelines I have seen. By observing conversations, he learned that listening involves:

1. Stating your intentions up front. Saying "I really want to understand what you have to say" or "I want to spend the next fifteen minutes just hearing your perspective"

creates clear expectations for the other person. Key to this is being authentically interested in learning what the other person has to say, which communicates a great deal nonverbally. As Durzo says, authenticity covers up a lot of sins.

2. Encouraging the other person to keep speaking. My favorite three words for this are "tell me more." You can also say:

> Oh?
>
> That's interesting.
>
> What else?
>
> Uh-huh.
>
> I'd like to hear more about that.
>
> Could you help me understand how you came to that decision?

3. Physically demonstrating that you are listening: nodding your head, smiling, using eye contact.

4. Confirming that you heard the person. This means summarizing and checking, as in, "So, if I understand you correctly, you think A, B, and C. Is that right?" or "So you are saying that X is important—or is there something I missed?"

Durzo also wrote about the importance of asking great questions. He coined the term "high-gain questions": those which motivated the other person to analyze, speculate, or express feelings.

To have the other person analyze, you might ask, "How has your thinking changed since 2016?" or "How would you compare that leader to the current leader?"

To ask the person to speculate, you could say, "If you could wave a magic wand, what would happen?" or "If you could pick one policy that mattered to you, what would it be?"

To encourage them to express feelings, you could ask, "How did you feel when you read that?" or "How would you describe your reaction to that debate?"

The questions that don't work for difficult exchanges are what I call "threatening questions," such as "Where the heck did you read *that*?" or "You don't really believe that's true, do you?" As Stefan Falk, a renowned executive coach and expert on brain psychology, reminded me, when we attack someone's core beliefs, we activate their amygdala, the part of their brain that centers on emotions like fear and anger. Everything related to logic and thinking—our frontal lobe—goes out the door. Make someone feel bad, and they will be convinced that you are wrong.

If you use the tools I just described to discuss a topic, conversations will flow, and you often will hear insights that you have never considered before.

Make no mistake: these conversations are not always easy. Sometimes you hear something so different from everything you believe that it's hard to say, "Tell me more."

In political communications, I often find:

- The person actually believes that your party or your candidate is equally guilty of what you accuse their side of doing. Examples of this are "I am okay with Trump's lies" (because all politicians lie, including Democrats), or "I am okay with socialist people in Congress who say extreme things" (because Republicans include radical conservatives who say awful things) or "I know you think that candidate is an egotistical sexual predator, but you have them in your party also."

- The person believes they have done extensive research into the issue—online and offline—and so the facts you cite don't resonate with them. Chances are, they have gotten their information from very different media sources from the ones you read. For instance, if you want to read about voter fraud, you can look at instances of fraud documented by the well-regarded conservative Heritage Foundation[5] and then move to One America News Network, where you can read dozens of articles about examples of fraud, from discrepancies in vote counts to problems with machines. Or you may find liberals who source their information starting from mainstream media and continuing with one-sided sites like Occupy Democrats. Many of the voters on my panel recounted spending hours going down a rabbit hole on a particular topic and often would support a controversial stand by saying, "I have done my homework on this issue."

- You hear a lot of comparisons that don't seem equivalent to you. For instance, you might hear a Trump supporter say that claims of fraud are similar to women who marched on Washington screaming "Not my president!" when Trump was elected in 2016. In these situations, it just doesn't matter if you believe the two situations are not comparable. Don't argue. Just realize that you are learning how "the other side" thinks.

In any situation, watching your language is really important. One of the main insights I have gotten from listening to voters is that we use labels as inaccurate and unfair stereotypes. We say "He's a Trumpster" instead of thinking about the whole person: that he is a husband and father and a really great store manager and a soccer coach and a generous community leader—and he also voted for

Trump. We don't need to agree with him, but it's a lot easier to listen if you regard someone as a whole human being.

One-on-one conversations are not the only action we can take. Lots of community and religious organizations have sponsored group versions of what Joseph and Aviva did: getting a dozen people together to spend time understanding each other's point of view. Some of us have seen this on television. The session starts with silence, mistrust, and a bit of dread. It ends with participants hugging each other.

These conversations built around hard listening work because success is about getting insight and understanding rather than about persuasion—at least in the beginning. And the upshot is often that we realize that "the other guys" become a source of learning that is more real and eye opening than we ever expected.

Irrationality

Don't expect people to be 100 percent rational. In fact, listening without lecturing works better because it helps avoid the "rationality trap." People are not always consistent and logical in their thinking. For instance, there is extensive research that proves that furnishing people with data doesn't convince them to change their minds. Dan Ariely, the behavioral economist, Duke professor, and co-founder of Irrational Capital, once told me that the world is filled with 8 billion irrational people. His book *Predictably Irrational* is brimming with examples of how people will take actions that defy logic, how our expectations affect our decisions, why golfers believe that everyone else cheats more than they do, why we buy items that are high priced, and even why calorie information has not motivated most people to eat healthier food. More recently, Ariely has spoken about how our mask-wearing habits are affected more by what others around us are doing rather than our own independent sense of what matters for our health.[6] Reading Ariely's work helped me understand my own irrationality, such as why I am against any kind of torture—and yet why I used to love watching the Fox show *24*, applauding with glee when the hero, Jack Bauer, beat up his prisoners. In the same way, people sometimes support candidates and policies for irrational reasons—such as a need to be part of a group—and all of the newspaper articles in the world will not change their minds.

In their landmark study, Hidden Tribes: A Study of America's Polarized Landscape, Stephen Hawkins, Daniel Yudkin, Míriam Juan-Torres, and Tim Dixon surveyed 8,000 Americans and ultimately identified seven "tribes": segments of voters with distinct beliefs and values.[7] Even among those tribes, however, it was clear that we humans are not consistent, rational thinkers. In one part of their research, for instance, the team learned that 81 percent of Americans believe that racism is a serious problem, but 85 percent believe that race should not be considered in college admissions decisions. It's difficult to see those statistics as rational, but at the core, people clearly don't define racism in the same way.

Stefan Falk, the executive coach, shared with me that humans in general don't like to think—that it goes back to caveman days and our need to conserve energy. Thinking is hard and as a result, humans love simple answers. We like quick explanations, one-liners, and uncomplicated truths. Why do I feel bad? Because my boss is a jerk. Why did I lose my job? It's all because of the immigrants. We need to work harder to go beyond the caveman brain and spend energy on listening, because it pays off in the long run. The right kind of conversation—filled with hard listening—helps us to dig deeper, gaining insight on why people feel the way they do, why we have irrational beliefs, and what the truth is behind our latest catchphrase.

How to Scale More Listening

The challenge is how to scale this notion of listening harder. Even if Joseph and Aviva and Doug and others who are open to this sort of listening each asked ten friends to do what they are doing, we would still cover only a tiny percentage of the US population. Still, just as videos go viral, this idea of taking a breath and trying to understand the other side could prove to be contagious. So, if the Joseph/Aviva/Doug friends group each find ten *more* friends to do this, we start to have a movement. In some sense, seeing is believing.

We can scale listening, then, by having better, less judgmental conversations and by watching these kinds of conversations with others. Video is a powerful medium for this. One extraordinary effort, by Jubilee Media, is a series called *Middle Ground*, in which the company brings together people from different sides of an issue for what founder Jason Lee calls "great dialogue and radical empathy." If you think Americans are politically polarized, just imagine the divide between Israelis and Palestinians. In 2018, Jubilee ran a moving session entitled "Can Israelis and Palestinians See Eye to Eye?," featuring young people from Israel and Palestine discussing their differences and common ground, giving hundreds of thousands of people an opportunity to fathom the issues in new ways.[8] It worked well to generate far more understanding and empathy. Organizations like Jubilee can create more of these conversations, and we can all watch and learn.

Despite what you may have heard about on-campus political correctness, breakthrough efforts to improve constructive intergroup dialogue are thriving at colleges and universities nationwide. According to Nancy Thomas, director of the Institute for Democracy & Higher Education (IDHE) at Tufts University's Tisch College of Civic Life, campuses are ideal locations for students to *practice* talking politics. IDHE works with 1,200 colleges and universities to improve student participation in democracy. The work includes helping faculty, staff, and students manage conflict, break down polarization, and discuss issues across difference. "Engaging in difficult discussions is not intuitive," says Thomas, "and many people simply avoid them. That is hurting democracy." She added, "We study and work to improve how people lead and engage in politically charged discussions." She has produced dozens of resources, such as classroom teaching tools, discussion materials, and a comprehensive guide for facilitating political dialogues.[9] Thomas advocates for a set of ground rules before any tricky conversations, to ensure learning, well-being, and success. Her list includes:

- Listen for understanding.
- Assume good will.
- Seek first to understand, and then to be understood.
- If you are offended or uncomfortable, say so, and say why.
- Share responsibility for making the discussion work.
- Share airtime.
- It's okay to disagree, but don't personalize.
- Speak for yourself, not for others.
- What's said here stays here.
- Check your positioning authority at the virtual door.
- Turn phones off.

There is also the case of Europe Talks, inspired by an experiment in the spring of 2019 by Zeit online, a major digital media company in Germany.[10] The team, led by Editor-in-Chief Jochen Wegner, matched 17,000 Europeans from 53 countries who all agreed to have a political argument with someone different from them. The project has morphed into an international platform that facilitates dialogue at scale.

A serious effort to scale "hard listening" won't succeed unless our most influential Americans jump onto the bandwagon. For instance, imagine MSNBC's Rachel Maddow looking into the camera and saying, "We are now going to suspend disbelief and try to understand those who disagree with our viewers." Even more, we need our president, our representatives in Congress, our governors, and our mayors to model the behavior they want to see in their constituents. Representative Cheri Bustos, one of only seven Democrats elected to Congress from a "Double Trump" district—a district that voted for Trump in both 2016 and 2020—told me that she attributes her victories to listening to her constituents and to making sure that "they understand that you *get* them."

Coupling conversation with experience can be the best way to find our common ground. In a post-COVID world, physically being with others will make a big difference. Visiting a community near the southern border of the US, for example, can be a transformational way to understand how people feel about immigration. Or, as Selena, a Democrat from Missouri, told me, "I went to the Range at St. Louis West, which is apparently one of the most advanced shooting ranges in the country—and I am embarrassed to say that it changed how I felt about guns. I had a blast."

Of course, one easy way to start finding our common ground is to just read about the other side, as you have done in this book. Hopefully, when you read about perspectives that seem downright crazy, you will stop and consider your own assumptions, the sources of your own data, and how that might differ from the data of others.

I have been in weekly conversation with voters across America for nearly five years. The most important thing I have learned is that sometimes, in the heat of the moment, we forget that we are all fellow Americans, that most of us are trying to get by and do our best, and that almost all are worthy of our respect and compassion. Walking in their shoes is a critical first step that can change the trajectory of our country in the 21st century.

Methodology

T he analysis in this book and the columns on which it is based comes from research activities I conducted with an online panel of American voters. This panel started in 2016 with 300 voters and eventually grew to 500 voters. The primary purpose of the panel is to engage with voters on an ongoing basis about their views of the country, the presidency, our politics, and the future. Although the size of the respondent base is sufficient for quantitative analysis, the primary objective of the project has been qualitative—to understand the "why" behind more quantitative methodologies like surveys and polls. In this situation, the design of the panel and its methodology had special considerations. First, candor was a critical factor: people are so used to being polled that many admit to not telling the truth to pollsters. And, given the divisiveness in our country, many voters are accustomed to avoiding controversy and keeping their opinions to themselves. Although it is not possible to guarantee that people would truthfully tell everything about what they were doing and thinking, we wanted to significantly increase the chances that this would happen.

Panelists were recruited via a variety of methods, including social media (recruiting from Facebook groups), in-person recruiting at political events, and purchases from firms that sell address-based sampling. We also added an incremental group of millennials in the summer of 2017 via work with the Blue Lab at the Liberty Square Group, a political consulting firm. We refresh the panel continuously, mostly to replace nonparticipants or to add segments of particular interest; for instance, in the summer of 2017, we added additional voters from Alabama in the midst of the Senate campaign with Roy Moore and Doug Jones. Since 2016, more than 1,000 voters have participated in the panel for some period of time.

As of December 31, 2020, the makeup of the panel was as follows:

- Democrats: 37%
- Republicans: 36%
- Independents: 27%
- Trump Voters (2016): 45%
- Clinton Voters (2016): 42%
- Nonvoters (2016): 4%
- Voted for other than Trump or Clinton (2016): 9%

Panelists represent all fifty states, with most states having ten participants. Exceptions to this include:

- Alabama: 11
- Alaska: 7
- Hawaii: 6
- Kansas: 9
- Massachusetts: 13
- Michigan: 14
- Mississippi: 6
- North Carolina: 12

- New Hampshire: 12
- North Dakota: 7
- Pennsylvania: 13
- Texas: 14
- Wyoming: 6

The demographics of the panel are as follows:

- Men: 231
- Women: 279
- White: 405
- African American or Caribbean American: 40
- Hispanic: 41
- Other: 16
- College graduates +:229
- Non–college grad: 271
- 18–29: 104
- 30–49: 143
- 50–64: 130
- 65+: 123

We based the decisions about numbers in each category above on many considerations. However, the primary driver was to get a critical mass of voters (focus group size) in each state and to generally reflect the other demographics of voters in the US.

To qualify members of the panel, we sent each prospective member a detailed description of the work, including guidelines ensuring that their privacy and confidentiality would be protected. In this document, I revealed that I had worked on an unpaid project for the Clinton campaign and that I was self-funding the research;

moreover, I noted that no organization was paying her for my data—to assure respondents that their opinions were not being "sold to the other side." If panelists wanted to continue, the next step was a 45-minute telephone interview with me, with the goal of verifying detailed demographic information (age, gender, occupation, location, voter registration, past presidential votes from 2008, 2012, and 2016, and so on). The second goal of the interview was to increase trust, so that participants would know that an actual person—who would only listen and not judge them—was on the other end of their comments. The third goal of the phone interviews was to make a determination about where along the political spectrum a respondent should be placed: liberal, moderate, or conservative. Moderates were tagged based on their views of where we are as a country and their reactions to certain questions about policy and values, including views on immigration, the media, health care, and gun control. All participants needed to have access to the internet. Approximately 90 percent of those interviewed qualified for the panel; those eliminated included non–US citizens and people who decided not to take the time to participate.

Once on the panel, participants are assigned weekly projects via email. These projects vary intentionally, to make participation fun and interesting, given the longitudinal nature of the work. Typical projects might be a true/false quiz, a video for people to view and respond to, a fill-in-the-blanks exercise (like Mad Libs), an open-ended question, a request that they ask questions of friends, or a request to watch a speech and send reactions. Additional techniques have included image annotation, voter journeys, mobile ethnography, and heat mapping. In rare circumstances, participants are given a more quantitative survey, but surveys are typically used to begin a conversation on a particular topic; for instance, people might be asked about whether they support Obamacare, but the focus of the response is on why they responded the way they did.

Other than bias that occasionally arises from sampling, the primary bias in this panel is that most of the respondents are more engaged politically than the average US citizen. Thus, for instance, they are much more likely to read a newspaper daily or to be aware of world events than a typical voter.

The responses are content coded and sorted, using spreadsheets and technology that was originally created at C Space for the purposes of coding qualitative content. Themes are ranked on a scale of 1-5, with 1 being "only said by one or two people" and 5 being "a major recurring theme." Quotes chosen for *Boston Globe* articles are typically rated a 4 or 5. From time to time, if I am unclear about a particular comment or response, I follow up with a phone call to the respondent.

None of the respondents are paid for their time. On average, a respondent will take five to ten minutes each week to do the work of the panel. Response rates are almost always greater than 50 percent and often significantly higher. The highest response rates come from fill-in-the-blanks/Mad Libs exercises.

At the end of 2020, I made a decision to end the panel, but hundreds of respondents continued to write to me. I decided to stay in touch with 150 voters to ensure that my data for this book was as accurate and current as possible.

The techniques I used were derived during my tenure as founder and CEO of Communispace Corporation, now C Space, which was acquired by Omnicom in 2011. Communispace was the first company to use online communities for market research, which is now an accepted and proven method of generating insight from the internet. In online communities, respondents are also able to have conversations with each other. In online panels, called communipanels, the respondents are only in conversation with the researcher. I chose panels because of the emotional nature of the

Acknowledgments

I t takes a village to create any book, but especially this one. From the summer of 2016 through February of 2021, more than one thousand American voters helped me to walk in their shoes. I never paid them for their perspectives, and yet hundreds of these people responded to my questions every week for years. They became friends, confidants, researchers, and observers for me, and they have inspired me to tell their stories. I have seen them go through deaths of family members, illness, births of children, divorce, marriage, hurricanes, tornadoes, mudslides, power outages, a brain tumor, a false missile alert, job loss, promotions, homelessness, COVID, and triumphs. One ran for state representative in his home state and won. Another is married to a Capitol Police officer. And they have reminded me that we are much more than who we vote for.

I am grateful to all of them, including those below who gave me permission to share their names:

Gary A. Adams	Nina M. Backon	Robert Borga
Danny Aguilar	Suzy Baker	Jeremy Branstad
Robin Albin	Selena Bauer	Lesa Rogers Broadhead
Chuck Allen	David Begley	Elizabeth Brown
Alden Applebee	Michelle Benko	James Brown
Dianne Arnheim	Jeff Bennett	Tanisha Brown
Joseph Arrambidez	Peter V.S. Bond	Alexander E. Jaramillo Burgos

Alexis Burke

Katrina Carus

John Chen

Karuna Chiemruom

Joe Clark

Ken Coogan

Lynn Corfield

Laura Dean

Kathryn Decker

Maxwell Dietz

Wil Dunn

David Edman

Jane Evelyn

Susan Farrell

Julia Feld

Barbara Krecker Fitchett

Jacqueline W. Garell

Adam Robert Geuss

Gretchen Glewwe

Laurence R. Golding

Victoria Gonzales

Tim Gray

Andrea Sussman Harris

Hakim Hassan

Julie Hayes

Sean Head

Jose Hernandez

Tim Hulsizer

Ernesto Humpierres

Hugh Jackson

Jim Jacobs

Reginald Jonas

Adam Johnson

David J. Kelley

Hugh Kelly

Tammy Kingston

Joel Kircher

Christopher Kril

Lawrence R. Kulig

Steve Kuttner

Allison T. LaFleur

Natalie Lalama

Ben Lewis

Mary Margaret Licisyn

Kevin M. Lynch

Colette Maillet

Patti Mansmann

Catherine Marenghi

Freddie Martin

Nicholas McCool

Dlana McEgan

Christina M. McGeough

Cecilia Milano

Susannah Miller

Bob Mumby

Lyn Nakashima

Susan Nardone

Sara Nelson

Shelly Nguyen

Selene Norman

Brenda Perry

Michael C. Pollock

Lynn Ricci

Lynnie Richey

Proncey D. Robertson

Nancy Ruffino

Katie Carus Ryan

Cindy Siagel

Katie Silva

Tom Slattery

Matthew Sliney

Yolanda Smith

Nicholas Spence

Gary Timmins

Thomas Tolman

Michael Tomaino

Brandon Tomayo

James S. Turner

Tracy Underwood

Caroline Wendricks

Andrew Westgate

Jowella Williams

Anne S. York

Jake Yost

It would be impossible for me to have found a better editor than Josh Bernoff. Josh and I have known each other for years. I religiously read his blog, *Without Bullshit*, and so it was easy for me to ask him to help me bring my research to life. He did so much more than fix my typos and grammar mistakes. Josh was my Sherpa, keeping me organized with spreadsheets and deadlines, helping me find resources, and pushing me hard. He was a candid and dedicated partner, with high standards, the ability to laugh right when I needed it, and great inspiration when I had writer's block.

The team at RealClear Publishing was enthusiastic about this journey from day one, and I am grateful for all of their support: Naren Aryal and Kristin Perry of Mascot Books and Carl Cannon of RealClear Politics were willing to make the entire process happen smoothly and rapidly, and we had a great time while doing it. Special thanks also to Lara Cavezza for being my web and design master for years, and to Stephani Finks for creating a book cover I love.

Understanding people who are different from me is my life's work, and in building Communispace (now C Space), I learned to take that passion and execute on it, developing technology for online communities and learning the secrets to getting people to open up and be engaged when we are not face to face. Thank you to everyone who helped to create this extraordinary company, but especially to the team members and clients who taught me the craft of bringing insights to life: Manila Austin, Tom Brailsford, Siobhan Dullea, Jim Figura, Rich Keller, Julie Wittes Schlack, Mel Seaborn, Stan Sthanunathan, and Gretchen Waitley.

I am blessed with wonderful friends who have supported this journey all along and who encouraged me to write this book. Some of them live far away, and yet they subscribed to the *Boston Globe* just to make sure they didn't miss my pieces. Others wrote me every time I had a column published. Some volunteered to read rough drafts of this book. Some brought me into their organizations to share what I was learning about voters. Some were just there whenever I needed a shoulder to lean on. I am especially grateful to my HBS Posse— Michael Bregman, Jocelyn Goldberg-Schaible, Alain Maurice, Steve

McConnell, and Joe Wald—who have encouraged me and been incredible lifelong friends and cheerleaders for all these years. Thank you also to Patricia and Jay Baitler, Ryan Barry, Beth Boland, Anne Bronner, Heather Campion, Karen Chaplin, Ruth Charny, Donna Chudacoff, Dana Cordova, Gail Deegan, Mindy Diamond, Eileen Edman, Steven Fischman, Carol and Bernie Fulp, Sol and Robyn Gittleman and the residents of Brookhaven, Gail Goodman, Wendy Grolnick, Jill Guz, Scott Harshbarger and Judy Stephenson, John and Pamela Humphrey, Cindy Jackson, Rosabeth Moss Kanter, Laurie Kaswiner, Steven Koltai, Judy Krandel, Pamela Lenehan, Bonnie Millender, Evelyn Murphy, Sue O'Connell, Lisa Ozer, Deval Patrick, Duncan Pollock and Karen Carhart, Maria and Marty Rapp, Jud and BB Reis, Jim Rooney, Len and Phyllis Schlesinger, Jack and Sandra Schwalb, Stacey Shuster, Laurie Slosberg, Alan Solomont, Jeffrey Sonnenfeld, David and Janet Soskin, Rabbi Keith Stern, Lindsay Sutton, Christina Thirkell, Amy Tonkonogy, Lauri Vinick, Gayle Wald, Heidi Wald, and Harvey and Linda Weiner. And my brother and sister, Howard and Jeri Hessan, were there every step of the way. Finally, Jen Reddy, as with everything else you do, you have gone above and beyond.

Joel Benenson, a brilliant strategist and pollster, was the friend who, after one long phone call, inspired me to take what I knew about helping brands understand consumers and apply it to the political realm. Special thanks also go to Scott Ferson of the Liberty Square Group, whose Blue Lab interns helped me recruit over 100 young voters to my research project.

When I wrote my first op-ed in 2016, I sent it to Linda Henry, who is now CEO of the *Boston Globe*—and Linda has encouraged me to keep going for years. I am grateful to her and to my fantastic Globe Opinion partner, Marjorie Pritchard, who worked with me on every column and kept the bar high. Thanks also to the three editorial page editors who have supported my work over the years: Ellen Clegg, Shirley Leung, and Bina Venkataraman.

Jake Tapper was the first television journalist to give my research national exposure, and to remind me that big things can come from people who grew up in the great Commonwealth of Pennsylvania.

Many political leaders reached out to me over the last four years wanting to learn more about my data. I am thankful for their excitement about my work. In particular, Governor Charlie Baker, former Massachusetts Congressman Joe Kennedy, Congressman Seth Moulton, and Congresswoman Cheri Bustos would write me, text me, and tell me what they wanted to know more about. To me, they modeled what we are looking for in our public servants.

I have the best daughters in the world. Despite their own challenges coping with work, child care, dog care, and more during COVID, Lindsay Garces and Amanda Garces reminded me constantly that I was making a difference. They edited my work, gave me feedback, and sat with me on Monday-evening Zoom calls about grammar, cover art, and layouts. They and their husbands, Noam Rifkind and Ryan Flood, are the reason it is all worthwhile. And to Bennett Flood: not a day goes by when you don't touch my heart, and I can't wait to meet your little sister.

My husband, Bob Stringer, author of four books himself, supported this project every moment of every day. When I thought about giving up, Bob told me I was crazy. When I wasn't sure what I wanted to say, Bob sat with my writing and scrawled all over every page. He was always in this 100 percent, and I cannot imagine this book—or life—without him.

Endnotes

1   Abel, David. "With fears of a contested election growing, more Americans stock up to ride out the discord." *Boston Globe*, October 23, 2020. https://www.bostonglobe.com/2020/10/23/nation/with-fears-contested-election-growing-more-americans-stock-up-ride-out-discord/

Part I

1   C-SPAN. "Campaign 2016: Harvard Campaign Manager's Panel," C-SPAN video, December 21, 2016. https://www.c-span.org/video/?419547-1/harvard-2016-presidential-campaign-managers-panel

2   Hessan, Diane. "Understanding the undecided voters." *Boston Globe*, November 21, 2016. https://www.bostonglobe.com/opinion/2016/11/21/understanding-undecided-voters/9EjNHVkt99b4re2VAB8ziI/story.html

3   Hessan, Diane. "Trump voters in the aftermath of Charlottesville." *Boston Globe*, August 21, 2017. https://www.bostonglobe.com/opinion/2017/08/21/trump-voters-aftermath-charlottesville/Z5v3vtum98hF25SRHulHKJ/story.html

4   Bernoff, Josh. "What are you actually DOING to fight racists and Nazis? Take the pro bono pledge." Without Bullshit, August 14, 2017. https://withoutbullshit.com/blog/actually-fight-racists-nazis-take-pro-bono-pledge

5   Jenkins, Aric. "Read President Trump's NFL Speech on National Anthem Protests." *TIME*, September 23, 2017. https://time.com/4954684/donald-trump-nfl-speech-anthem-protests/

6   Hessan, Diane. "Why Trump voters want to boycott the NFL." *Boston Globe*, September 28, 2017. https://www.bostonglobe.com/opinion/2017/09/28/why-trump-voters-want-boycott-nfl/QjYBXqROjM5QsXZXMY1mCK/story.html

7   Kerr, Steve (as told to Chris Ballard). "Mr. President: You Represent All of Us. Don't Divide Us. Bring Us Together." *Sports Illustrated*, September 24, 2017. https://www.si.com/nba/2017/09/24/steve-kerr-warriors-donald-trump-white-house-stephen-curry

8   Hessan, Diane. "The view from Alabama: Why Roy Moore will win." *Boston Globe*, December 7, 2017. https://www.bostonglobe.com/opinion/2017/12/07/the-view-from-alabama-why-roy-moore-will-win/bMorqGhRAM6DBtTQR2OP6N/story.html

9   McCrummen, Stephanie, Beth Reinhard, and Alice Crites. "Woman says Roy Moore initiated sexual encounter when she was 14, he was 32." *The Washington Post*, November 9, 2017. https://www.washingtonpost.com/investigations/woman-says-roy-moore-initiated-sexual-encounter-when-she-was-14-he-was-32/2017/11/09/1f495878-c293-11e7-afe9-4f60b5a6c4a0_story.html

10   McCrummen, Stephanie, Beth Reinhard, and Alice Crites. "Two more women describe unwanted overtures by Roy Moore at Alabama mall." *The Washington Post*, November 15, 2017. https://www.washingtonpost.com/investigations/two-more-women-describe-unwanted-overtures-by-roy-moore-at-alabama-mall/2017/11/15/2a1da432-ca24-11e7-b0cf-7689a9f2d84e_story.html

11   Hessan, Diane. "Voters on Iran: A split decision." *Boston Globe*, May 18, 2018. https://www.bostonglobe.com/opinion/2018/05/17/voters-iran-split-decision/vrwyIk0goy1oQml7tGUBbK/story.html

12   Hessan, Diane. "Kavanaugh nomination has turned into a circus." *Boston Globe*, September 25, 2018. https://www.bostonglobe.com/opinion/2018/09/25/under-big-top-supreme-court-hysteria/vb9I14ryyh1jTvqeVXNq7H/story.html

13   "WTAS: Support for President Donald J. Trump's Nomination of Judge Brett Kavanaugh to the Supreme Court." Archive of Trump-era Whitehouse.gov, July 9, 2018. https://trumpwhitehouse.archives.gov/briefings-statements/wtas-support-president-donald-j-trumps-nomination-judge-brett-kavanaugh-supreme-court/

14   Morin, Rebecca. "Trump triples down on his controversial tweets about 'The Squad.' Here's what we know." *USA Today*, July 15, 2019. https://www.usatoday.com/story/news/politics/2019/07/15/trumps-tweets-the-squad-heres-what-we-know/1736706001/

15   Hessan, Diane. "Trump vs. the Squad—voters weigh in." *Boston Globe*, July 18, 2019. https://www.bostonglobe.com/opinion/2019/07/18/trump-squad-voters-weigh/gDMjGnjwi0YgFytIx6JTgJ/story.html

16   RT (Russia Today). "ICE protesters take down American flag & replace it with Mexican one." RT [Russia Today], July 16, 2019. https://www.youtube.com/watch?v=zrG1XY2RkKU

17   Hessan, Diane. "The nation is in crisis. Where are you, Joe Biden?" *Boston Globe*, April 22, 2020. https://www.bostonglobe.com/2020/04/22/opinion/nation-is-crisis-where-are-you-joe-biden/

18   Sinozich, Sofi. "Biden consolidates support, but trails badly in enthusiasm: Poll." ABC News, March 29, 2020. https://abcnews.go.com/Politics/biden-consolidates-support-trails-badly-enthusiasm-poll/story?id=69812092

19   "Who's ahead in the national polls?" Fivethirtyeight.com aggregation of 2020 presidential election polls. https://projects.fivethirtyeight.com/polls/president-general/national/

20   Hessan, Diane. "Voters weigh in on the debate: Trump lost the night." *Boston Globe*, October 1, 2020. https://www.bostonglobe.com/2020/10/01/opinion/voters-weigh-debate-trump-lost-night/

21   Cook, Sara. "Election infrastructure officials: 2020 election was 'most secure in American history.'" CBS News, November 12, 2020. https://www.cbsnews.com/live-updates/2020-election-most-secure-history-dhs/#post-update-40aa9fd8

22   Cummings, William, Joey Garrison, and Jim Sergent. "By the numbers: President Donald Trump's failed efforts to overturn the election." *USA Today*, January 6, 2021. https://www.usatoday.com/in-depth/news/politics/elections/2021/01/06/trumps-failed-efforts-overturn-election-numbers/4130307001/

23   Link, Devon, and Ashley Nerbovig. "Fact check: Videos showing crowd locked out of Detroit TCF Center with windows obstructed are missing context." *USA Today*, November 10, 2020. https://www.usatoday.com/story/news/factcheck/2020/11/10/fact-check-videos-crowd-locked-out-detroit-center-lack-context/6195038002/

24   Alberta, Tim. "A Journey Into the Heart of America's Voting Paranoia." *Politico Magazine*, October 30, 2020. https://www.politico.com/news/magazine/2020/10/30/voting-mail-election-2020-paranoia-433356

25   McCarthy, Justin. "Confidence in Accuracy of U.S. Election Matches Record Low." Gallup.com, October 8, 2020. https://news.gallup.com/poll/321665/confidence-accuracy-election-matches-record-low.aspx

26   Silverstein, Jason. "Cuomo says Trump 'better have an army' to walk down the streets of NYC." CBS News, September 4, 2020. https://www.cbsnews.com/news/andrew-cuomo-trump-threat-new-york-city-funding/

27   Axelrod, Tal. "Pelosi says Dems 'have to be ready to throw a punch—for the children' in 2020." *The Hill*, August 23, 2019. https://thehill.com/homenews/house/458594-pelosi-says-dems-have-to-be-ready-to-throw-a-punch-for-the-children-in-2020

28   "Madonna: 'Thought About Blowing up White House.'" AP News, January 22, 2017. https://apnews.com/article/616edfeb9a034b0ba435cf9f774970a4

29   Hains, Tim. "Dem Rep. Ted Lieu Predicts 'Widespread Civil Unrest' If Trump Fires Mueller." RealClearPolitics.com, March 20, 2018. https://www.realclearpolitics.com/video/2018/03/20/dem_rep_ted_lieu_predicts_widespread_civil_unrest_if_trump_fires_mueller.html

30   Hayes, Christal. "Eric Holder says Michelle Obama was wrong: 'When they go low, we kick them.'" *USA Today*, October 10, 2018. https://www.usatoday.com/story/news/politics/onpolitics/2018/10/10/eric-holder-says-michelle-obama-wrong-when-they-go-low-we-kick-them/1593189002/

Part II

1 Walters, Joanna. "NRA lawsuit: who are the four leaders accused of corruption?" *The Guardian*, August 6, 2020. https://www.theguardian.com/us-news/2020/aug/06/nra-accused-corruption-wayne-lapierre-wilson-phillips-joshua-powell-john-frazer

2 Linton, Caroline. "Biden calls on Congress to ban assault weapons and institute other gun restrictions." CBS News, February 15, 2021. https://www.cbsnews.com/news/biden-urges-gun-law-reforms-on-parkland-shooting-anniversary/

3 Hessan, Diane. "Finding common ground on gun control." *Boston Globe*, October 27, 2017. https://www.bostonglobe.com/opinion/2017/10/27/finding-common-ground-gun-control/I0SsZjmE75N36iJH0DdzDK/story.html

4 Quinnipiac University Polling. "U.S. Voter Support For Gun Control At All-Time High, Quinnipiac University National Poll Finds; Trump Helped Texas, Florida, Not Puerto Rico, Voters Say." Quinnipiac University Poll, October 12, 2017. https://poll.qu.edu/national/release-detail?ReleaseID=2492

5 Hessan, Diane. "The problem isn't how we feel about Trump—it's how we feel about each other." *Boston Globe*, July 18, 2018. https://www.bostonglobe.com/opinion/2018/07/18/the-problem-isn-how-feel-about-trump-how-feel-about-each-other/G123Ce0gLHtACdF4wyyqmN/story.html

6 Hessan, Diane. "Immigration—the problem Congress doesn't want to solve." *Boston Globe*, December 10, 2018. https://www.bostonglobe.com/opinion/2018/12/10/immigration-problem-congress-doesn-want-solve/aR2QxaPxgxSH7xQfX8GKyL/story.html

7 Hessan, Diane. "Climate change will be a decisive issue in 2020." *Boston Globe*, June 26, 2019. https://www.bostonglobe.com/opinion/2019/06/26/climate-change-will-decisive-issue/OlE9mWwCBZD1lbqSxi3CmI/story.html

8 Bach, Natasha. "Michael Bloomberg Pledges $500 Million to Combat Climate Change." *Fortune*, June 7, 2019. https://fortune.com/2019/06/07/michael-bloomberg-climate-change/

9 Our Children's Trust. "Youth v. Gov.: Juliana v. US" in OurChildrensTrust.org. https://www.ourchildrenstrust.org/juliana-v-us

10 Evich, Helena Bottemiller. "Agriculture Department buries studies showing dangers of climate change." Politico, June 23, 2019. https://www.politico.com/story/2019/06/23/agriculture-department-climate-change-1376413

11 Hessan, Diane. "Our continental divide." *Boston Globe*, December 4, 2019. https://www.bostonglobe.com/2019/12/04/opinion/our-continental-divide/

12 Trump, Donald. Archived at Trump Twitter Archive, originally tweeted by @realDonaldTrump on September 30, 2019. https://www.thetrumparchive.com/?searchbox=%22rep.+adam+schiff+illegally%22

13   Paschal, Olivia. "John McCain's Final Letter to America." *The Atlantic*, August 27, 2018. https://www.theatlantic.com/ideas/archive/2018/08/john-mccains-final-letter-to-america/568669/

14   Denne, Luke and Charlotte Gardiner. "Former U.S. officials criticize Trump's decision to 'abandon' Kurds." NBC News, November 17, 2019. https://www.nbcnews.com/news/world/former-u-s-officials-criticize-trump-s-decision-abandon-kurds-n1084156

15   Harris, Shane, Greg Miller, and Josh Dawsey. "CIA concludes Saudi crown prince ordered Jamal Khashoggi's assassination." *The Washington Post*, November 16, 2018. https://www.washingtonpost.com/world/national-security/cia-concludes-saudi-crown-prince-ordered-jamal-khashoggis-assassination/2018/11/16/98c89fe6-e9b2-11e8-a939-9469f1166f9d_story.html

16   Amadeo, Kimberly. "Who Owns the US National Debt." The Balance, March 2, 2021. https://www.thebalance.com/who-owns-the-u-s-national-debt-3306124

17   Hessan, Diane. "When voters hear about foreign policy, they yawn." *Boston Globe*, December 27, 2019. https://www.bostonglobe.com/2019/12/27/opinion/when-voters-hear-about-foreign-policy-they-yawn/

18   Rubin, Jennifer. "Joe Biden's big foreign policy speech." *The Washington Post*, July 11, 2019. https://www.washingtonpost.com/opinions/2019/07/11/joe-bidens-big-foreign-policy-speech/

19   "What Issues Should The 2020 Democratic Candidates Be Talking About?" Fivethirtyeight.com, September 18, 2019. https://fivethirtyeight.com/features/what-issues-should-the-2020-democratic-candidates-be-talking-about/

20   Rogin, Josh. "133 foreign policy officials endorse Joe Biden." *The Washington Post*, November 12, 2019. https://www.washingtonpost.com/opinions/2019/11/12/foreign-policy-officials-endorse-joe-biden/

21   Fearnow, Benjamin. "Fox News Poll: 54 Percent of Americans Say Trump Should Be Impeached." *Newsweek*, December 15, 2019. https://www.newsweek.com/fox-news-poll-majority-americans-support-impeaching-donald-trump-removed-office-1477340

22   Concha, Jose. "3 reasons why impeachment fatigue has already set in." *The Hill*, November 18, 2109. https://thehill.com/opinion/white-house/470947-3-reasons-why-impeachment-fatigue-has-already-set-in

23   Ibid.

24   Sergeant, Jacqueline. "Many Americans Struggle To Make Ends Meet Despite Growing Economy." *Financial Advisor Magazine*, July 3, 2019. https://www.fa-mag.com/news/many-americans-struggle-to-make-ends-meet-despite-growing-economy-45765.html

25 Konish, Lorie. "137 million Americans are struggling with medical debt. Here's what to know if you need some relief." CNBC, November 10, 2019. https://www.cnbc.com/2019/11/10/americans-are-drowning-in-medical-debt-what-to-know-if-you-need-help.html

26 Hessan, Diane. "It's still the economy, stupid." *Boston Globe*, March 2, 2020. https://www.bostonglobe.com/2020/03/01/opinion/its-still-economy-stupid/

27 Rosenberg, Eli, and Heather Long. "The economy added 225,000 jobs in January, showing continued strength." *The Washington Post*, February 7, 2020. https://www.washingtonpost.com/business/2020/02/07/february-2020-jobs-report/

28 Maloney, Christopher, and Adam Tempkin. "America's Middle Class Is Addicted to a New Kind of Credit." Bloomberg News, October 29, 2019. https://www.bloomberg.com/news/articles/2019-10-29/america-s-middle-class-is-getting-hooked-on-debt-with-100-rates

Part III

1 Hessan, Diane. "The insults of our president." *Boston Globe*, January 15, 2018. https://www.bostonglobe.com/opinion/2018/01/15/the-insults-our-president/WiZWsFMugKbz3qKZ9ehncK/story.html

2 Harrington, Rebecca. "Here's what Trump means when he says 'drain the swamp'— even though it's not an accurate metaphor." Business Insider, November 12, 2016. https://www.businessinsider.in/Heres-what-Trump-means-when-he-says-drain-the-swamp-even-though-its-not-an-accurate-metaphor/articleshow/55381013.cms

3 Hessan, Diane. "The muck and mud in Washington—how voters see it." *Boston Globe*, February 7, 2018. https://www.bostonglobe.com/opinion/2018/02/07/the-muck-and-mud-washington-how-voters-see/hXCNbQxUcIHMoO0fYXBLmN/story.html

4 Hessan, Diane. "Does Trump's character count?" *Boston Globe*, June 9, 2019. https://www.bostonglobe.com/opinion/2019/06/09/does-trump-character-count/jRP8mEQfnTbXMDSAbgWUeN/story.html

5 "How unpopular is Donald Trump." Aggregation of ratings over time by Fivethirtyeight.com. https://projects.fivethirtyeight.com/trump-approval-ratings/

6 Hessan, Diane. "Joe Biden's humanity could be his edge in 2020." *Boston Globe*, August 9, 2018. https://www.bostonglobe.com/opinion/2018/08/09/joe-biden-humanity-could-his-edge/v41lXHG9vuEfCc0Ri805LL/story.html

7 Cillizza, Chris, and Harry Enten. "The definitive ranking of 2020 Democrats." CNN, July 20, 2018. https://www.cnn.com/2018/07/19/politics/2020-democrats-rankings/index.html

8 Shear, Michael D. "Vice President Biden's son Beau dies of brain cancer." *Boston Globe*, May 31, 2015. https://www.bostonglobe.com/news/nation/2015/05/30/vice-president-biden-son-beau-dies-brain-cancer/iOUNcVHNRpcZqaj2c4TrqK/story.html

9   Sherman, Mark, and Jessica Gresko. "Ruth Bader Ginsburg signals she won't retire soon." *Boston Globe*, January 27, 2018. https://www3.bostonglobe.com/news/politics/2018/01/27/ruth-bader-ginsburg-and-liberal-icon-supreme-court-signals-she-won-retire-soon/qcAsrllate4SXkGftiFokO/story.html

10   Freyer, Felice J., and Janelle Nanos. "Bezos, Buffett, Dimon health venture will be based in Boston." *Boston Globe*, June 20, 2018. https://www3.bostonglobe.com/business/2018/06/20/gawande/C7uFtpyQ9DDpqNZ6BvA35J/story.html

11   Kessler, Glenn. "Trump made 30,573 false or misleading claims as president. Nearly half came in his final year." *The Washington Post*, January 23, 2021. https://www.washingtonpost.com/politics/how-fact-checker-tracked-trump-claims/2021/01/23/ad04b69a-5c1d-11eb-a976-bad6431e03e2_story.html

12   Hessan, Diane. "Playing the integrity card." *Boston Globe*, November 1, 2019. https://www.bostonglobe.com/opinion/2019/11/01/playing-integrity-card/y8wjh8xy71NcuGuH0hA3DJ/story.html

13   Elkins, Kathleen. "Bill Clinton says he left the White House $16 million in debt." CNBC, June 5, 2018. https://www.cnbc.com/2018/06/04/the-clintons-erased-16-million-in-debt-and-accumulated-45-million.html

14   Rogers, Katie. "Obamas Pay $8.1 Million for Home Just Miles From White House." *The New York Times*, May 31, 2017. https://www.nytimes.com/2017/05/31/us/obama-buys-house-washington-kalorama.html

15   Hood, Bryan. "Barack and Michelle Obama Are About to Buy This Sprawling $15 Million Martha's Vineyard Estate." *Robb Report*, August 23, 2019. https://robbreport.com/shelter/homes-for-sale/obamas-marthas-vineyard-estate-15-million-2865341/

16   Re, Gregg. "Graham lashes out at impeachment inquiry: 'If we were doing this, you'd be beating the sh-- out of us.'" Fox News, October 24, 2019. https://www.foxnews.com/politics/graham-resolution-condemning-impeachment-inquiry-lashes-out

17   McDonald, Danny, and Travis Andersen. "California businessman sentenced to 4 months in prison in college admissions scandal." *Boston Globe*, September 24, 2019. https://www.bostonglobe.com/metro/2019/09/24/dad-who-paid-get-son-admitted-usc-water-polo-star-faces-sentencing-college-admissions-scandal/6bJbEIR5DNtnQf35Eo5sNP/story.html

18   Hessan, Diane. "Who are the maskless people." *Boston Globe*, August 3, 2020. https://www.bostonglobe.com/2020/08/03/opinion/who-is-making-mask-rules/

19   Rivas, Karolina, and Angeline Jane Bernabe. "Video of woman's tirade after refusing to wear a mask in Trader Joe's goes viral." ABC News, June 29, 2020. https://abcnews.go.com/GMA/News/video-womans-tirade-refusing-wear-mask-trader-joes/story?id=71505060

20   Lin, Summer. "Woman kicked off plane for not wearing face mask—and passengers applaud, video shows." *Miami Herald*, July 24, 2020. https://www.miamiherald.com/news/coronavirus/article244475232.html

21   Schultz, Marisa. "Fauci urges governments to be 'as forceful as possible' on mask rules." Fox News, July 17, 2020. https://www.foxnews.com/politics/fauci-urges-governments-to-be-as-forceful-as-possible-on-mask-rules

22   Brenan, Megan. "Americans' Face Mask Usage Varies Greatly by Demographics." Gallup, July 13, 2020. https://news.gallup.com/poll/315590/americans-face-mask-usage-varies-greatly-demographics.aspx

23   Vazquez, Maegan, Dana Bash, and Kaitlan Collins. "Trump tweets image of himself wearing a mask and calls it 'patriotic.'" CNN, July 20, 2020. https://www.cnn.com/2020/07/20/politics/donald-trump-mask-tweet/index.html

Part IV

1   "List of post-2016 election Donald Trump rallies." Wikipedia.org, retrieved March 9, 2021. https://en.wikipedia.org/wiki/List_of_post-2016_election_Donald_Trump_rallies

2   Hessan, Diane. "Trump and the rally culture." *Boston Globe*, April 12, 2017. https://www.bostonglobe.com/opinion/2017/04/12/trump-and-rally-culture/dViwdabFWw2zdFfD1tBcVP/story.html

3   Gallup. "Presidential Job Approval Center." Gallup, compiled over time. https://news.gallup.com/interactives/185273/presidential-job-approval-center.aspx

4   Decker, Cathleen. "Trump leaves the White House bubble and shifts to campaign mode, hoping for momentum." *Los Angeles Times*, February 17, 2017. https://www.latimes.com/politics/la-na-pol-trump-rally-20170217-story.html

5   Hessan, Diane. "Patriots for Trump." *Boston Globe*, August 1, 2017. https://www.bostonglobe.com/opinion/2017/08/01/patriots-for-trump/DR3Yvz9Bx0uojz3knTe3BN/story.html

6   Stack, Liam. "Boy Scouts apologize for Trump's remarks at jamboree." *Boston Globe*, July 27, 2017. https://www.bostonglobe.com/news/politics/2017/07/27/boy-scouts-apologize-over-trump-remarks-jamboree/Lf32fJS6yK9LaeWodRz5QK/story.html

7   Hessan, Diane, and Josh Bernoff. "Fake news, real consequences." *Boston Globe*, September 13, 2019. https://www.bostonglobe.com/opinion/2019/09/13/fake-news-real-consequences/ocn0ouCybfL4qNb1YAeFcK/story.html

8   Chang, Juju, Jake Lefferman, Claire Pederson, and Geoff Martz. "When Fake News Stories Make Real News Headlines." ABC News. November 29, 2016. https://abcnews.go.com/Technology/fake-news-stories-make-real-news-headlines/story?id=43845383

9   Bernoff, Josh. "The truth matters more than which party you support." Withoutbullshit.com, April 13, 2018. https://withoutbullshit.com/blog/the-truth-matters-more-than-which-party-you-support

10   LaCapria, Kim. "Did Donald Trump Say Community College Is '13th Grade' for 'Dummys'?" Snopes.com, April 6, 2018. https://www.snopes.com/fact-check/did-trump-say-community-college-13th-grade/

11   O'Sullivan, Donie. "The Democratic Party deepfaked its own chairman to highlight 2020 concerns." CNN, August 10, 2019. https://www.cnn.com/2019/08/09/tech/deepfake-tom-perez-dnc-defcon/index.html

12   Penn, Christopher S. "Great Power, Great Responsibility: AI and Elections." Christopher S. Penn (blog), May 13, 2019. https://www.christopherspenn.com/2019/05/great-power-great-responsibility-ai-elections/

13   Garrett, R. Kelly, Robert Bond, and Shannon Poulsen. "Maybe you know that article is satire, but a lot of people can't tell the difference." Nieman Lab, August 19, 2019. https://www.niemanlab.org/2019/08/maybe-you-know-that-article-is-satire-but-a-lot-of-people-cant-tell-the-difference/

14   Hern, Alex. "Mark Zuckerberg's remarks on Holocaust denial 'irresponsible.'" *The Guardian*, July 19, 2018. https://www.theguardian.com/technology/2018/jul/19/mark-zuckerberg-holocaust-denial-facebook-remarks-offensive

15   "US election 2020: What do polls say about Trump v Biden?" Compilation of polls by RealClearPolitics on BBC.com. https://www.bbc.com/news/election-us-2020-54094119

16   Sargent, Greg. "Why did Democrats bleed House seats? A top analyst offers surprising answers." *The Washington Post*, November 27, 2020. https://www.washingtonpost.com/opinions/2020/11/27/why-did-democrats-bleed-house-seats-top-analyst-offers-surprising-answers/

17   Hessan, Diane. "The problem with polling." *Boston Globe*, November 13, 2020. https://www.bostonglobe.com/2020/11/13/opinion/problem-with-polling/?event=event12

18   Metz, Cade. "Study considers a link between QAnon and polling errors." *Boston Globe*, November 6, 2020. https://www.bostonglobe.com/2020/11/06/nation/study-considers-link-between-qanon-polling-errors/

Part V

1   Hessan, Diane. "It's my (political) party and I'll cry if I want to." *Boston Globe*, December 3, 2017. https://www.bostonglobe.com/opinion/2017/12/03/political-party-and-cry-want/fMpqpez4snQLRfxx1dDR2K/story.html

2   Hessan, Diane. "Need a blue wave? Twisting and shouting won't work." *Boston Globe*, June 20, 2018. https://www.bostonglobe.com/opinion/2018/06/20/need-blue-wave-twisting-and-shouting-won-work/QukLqaXdcJMZrCW8zkxc5I/story.html

3   Hessan, Diane. "Making waves in the Democratic Party." *Boston Globe*, October 24, 2018. https://www.bostonglobe.com/opinion/2018/10/24/making-waves-democratic-party/TxKFnrqpcueUIhSO8Z07AP/story.html

4   Hawkins, Stephen, Daniel Yudkin, Juan-Torres, Miriam, and Tom Dixon. "Hidden Tribes: A Study of America's Polarized Landscape." Report published 2018 by More in Common. Available at https://hiddentribes.us/

5   Greer, Simon. "Andrew Gillum, Florida's possible next governor, has the winning message for Democrats." Salon.com, October 19, 2018. https://www.salon.com/2018/10/19/why-floridas-possible-next-governor-andrew-gillum-has-a-winning-message-for-democrats_partner/

6   Hessan, Diane. "Trump or a radical socialist in 2020? Take your pick." *Boston Globe*, March 13, 2019. https://www.bostonglobe.com/opinion/2019/03/13/trump-radical-socialist-take-your-pick/8MenhORTqJtmKtlnwT6J2O/story.html

7   Pfannenstiel, Brianne. "Iowa caucus 2020: Inside the Iowa Democratic Party's 'boiler room,' where 'hell' preceded the results catastrophe." *Des Moines Register*, February 8, 2020. https://www.desmoinesregister.com/story/news/elections/presidential/caucus/2020/02/08/iowa-caucus-2020-inside-democrats-chaotic-call-center-boiler-room/4690263002/

8   Hessan, Diane. "Fear and loathing in the Democratic Party." *Boston Globe*, February 6, 2020. https://www.bostonglobe.com/2020/02/06/opinion/fear-loathing-democratic-party/

9   Nicholas, Peter. "Donald Trump Has One Problem." *The Atlantic*, January 23, 2020. https://www.theatlantic.com/politics/archive/2020/01/white-house-chaos-and-trump-credibility-crisis/605380/

10   Fearnow, Benjamin. "RNC Says Iowa Caucuses Are Proof 'Democrats Can't Run Our Country.'" *Newsweek*, February 4, 2020. https://www.newsweek.com/rnc-says-iowa-caucuses-are-proof-democrats-cant-run-our-country-1485704

11   Gallup. "Party Affiliation." Gallup, compilation over time. https://news.gallup.com/poll/15370/party-affiliation.aspx

Part VI

1   Pew Research Center. "Political Independents: Who They Are, What They Think." Report published March 2019. Available at https://www.pewresearch.org/politics/2019/03/14/political-independents-who-they-are-what-they-think/

2   Hessan, Diane. "Meet the New Independents." *Boston Globe*, July 10, 2017. https://www.bostonglobe.com/opinion/2017/07/10/meet-new-independents/VnpV8WOfibCpGbLIiZ9M5O/story.html

3   "National Exit Polls: How Different Groups Voted." *The New York Times*, 2020 election coverage. https://www.nytimes.com/interactive/2020/11/03/us/elections/exit-polls-president.html

4   Hessan, Diane. "About those 'Women for Trump.'" *Boston Globe*, January 24, 2020. https://www.bostonglobe.com/2020/01/24/opinion/about-those-women-trump/

5   Trump, Donald. Archived at Trump Twitter Archive, originally tweeted by @realDonaldTrump on January 20, 2020. https://www.thetrumparchive.com/?searchbox=%22Two+stone+cold+losers%22

6   Hessan, Diane. "Disillusioned Trump voters—up for grabs." *Boston Globe*, May 29, 2020. https://www.bostonglobe.com/2020/05/29/opinion/disillusioned-trump-voters-up-grabs/

7   Trump, Donald. Archived at Trump Twitter Archive, originally tweeted by @realDonaldTrump on May 12, 2020. https://www.thetrumparchive.com/?searchbox=%22When+will+they+open+a+Cold+Case%22

8   Hessan, Diane. "It's past time for white people to step up." *Boston Globe*, June 19, 2020. https://www.bostonglobe.com/2020/06/19/opinion/its-past-time-white-people-step-up/

9   Circle Center for Information & Research on Civic Learning and Engagement. "Election Week 2020: Young People Increase Turnout, Lead Biden to Victory." Circle/Tufts Tisch College, November 25, 2020. https://circle.tufts.edu/latest-research/election-week-2020#youth-voter-turnout-increased-in-2020

10   Ibid.

11   Hessan, Diane. "Young people, get out your vote." *Boston Globe*, October 16, 2020. https://www.bostonglobe.com/2020/10/16/opinion/young-people-get-out-your-vote/

12   Circle Center for Information & Research on Civic Learning and Engagement. "2020 Election Center." Circle/Tufts Tisch College. https://circle.tufts.edu/2020-election-center

13   Circle Center for Information & Research on Civic Learning and Engagement. "The Youth Vote on Super Tuesday." Circle/Tufts Tisch College, March 3, 2020. https://circle.tufts.edu/latest-research/super-tuesday-2020

14   Circle Center for Information & Research on Civic Learning and Engagement. "2020 Election Center." Circle/Tufts Tisch College. https://circle.tufts.edu/2020-election-center

15   Carmichael, Sarah Green. "Millennials Are Actually Workaholics, According to Research." *Harvard Business Review*, August 17, 2016. https://hbr.org/2016/08/millennials-are-actually-workaholics-according-to-research

Part VII

1   Arrambidez, Joseph. "The media and social platforms divide us." *Boston Globe*, November 16, 2020. https://www.bostonglobe.com/2020/11/16/opinion/unite-we-cant-even-have-civil-debate/

2   Brooks, Aviva. "An invitation, for real, to bridge our political divide." *Boston Globe* (letter to the editor), November 21, 2020. https://www.bostonglobe.com/2020/11/21/opinion/between-we-they-there-is-american-challenge-that-is-us/

3   Brooks, Aviva. "Political opposites find common ground, and hope, in one-to-one exchanges." *Boston Globe* (letter to the editor), February 1, 2021. https://www.bostonglobe.com/2021/02/01/opinion/path-unity-begins-most-basic-personal-level/

4   Ibid.

5   The Heritage Foundation. "A Sampling of Recent Election Fraud Cases from Across the United States." Undated compilation. https://www.heritage.org/voterfraud

6   Ariely, Dan. "Ask Ariely: On Philanthropic Freebies, Missing Masks, and Behavioral Biases." Dan Ariely blog, August 22, 2020. https://danariely.com/2020/08/22/ask-ariely-on-philanthropic-freebies-missing-masks-and-behavioral-biases/

7   Hawkins, Stephen, Daniel Yudkin, Juan-Torres, Miriam, and Tom Dixon. "Hidden Tribes: A Study of America's Polarized Landscape," p. 98. Report published 2018 by More in Common. Available at https://hiddentribes.us/

8   Jubilee. "Can Israelis and Palestinians See Eye to Eye? || Creators for Change | Middle Ground." Jubilee YouTube channel, November 12, 2018. https://www.youtube.com/watch?v=_Jj8vne0ca0

9   Thomas, Nancy, and Mark Brimhall-Vargas. "Facilitating Political Discussions." Tufts Institute for Democracy & Higher Education. Available at https://idhe.tufts.edu/resource/facilitating-political-discussions-facilitator-training-workshop-guide

10   Wegner, Jochen. "What happened when we paired up thousands of strangers to talk politics." TED, July 2019. https://www.ted.com/talks/jochen_wegner_what_happened_when_we_paired_up_thousands_of_strangers_to_talk_politics?language=en

Index

About the Author

Diane Hessan is an award-winning entrepreneur and innovator in the market research field, and a nationally recognized expert on the American voter. Since 2016, she has been engaged in an in-depth, longitudinal study of the electorate, looking for trends, shifts, and common ground. She has written more than 50 columns about her findings for the *Boston Globe*, and her work has also been featured on CNN and NPR and in the *Wall Street Journal*, the *New York Times*, *Forbes*, *Fortune*, and many other outlets.

She is the founder and Chairman of C Space, formerly called Communispace, which was the first company to leverage social media to help companies get insight and inspiration from their consumers. Diane was CEO of the company during 14 years of exponential growth, as C Space worked with hundreds of global brands across twelve countries. She has been honored as a disruptor in the market research industry because of her work in conducting breakthrough research via the internet. Diane recently consolidated all of her investment and advisory work into a new company called Salient Ventures, which helps accelerate the next generation of startup companies in tech.

She serves on the boards of Panera, Eastern Bank, Brightcove, Schlesinger Group, Mass Challenge, Tufts University, and Beth Israel

Deaconess Medical Center. In 2017, the Boston Globe appointed her to its editorial board. Diane has received many honors, including the Pinnacle Award from the Greater Boston Chamber of Commerce, the Most Admired CEO award and Boston Power 50 awards from the *Boston Business Journal*, Ernst & Young's Entrepreneur of the Year, the Northstar Award from Springboard, and the Greater Boston Chamber of Commerce Entrepreneur of the Year. She has been inducted into the Babson College Academy of Distinguished Entrepreneurs, and she received the Asper Award for Global Entrepreneurship from Brandeis University.

Diane previously co-authored the book *Customer-Centered Growth: Five Strategies for Building Competitive Advantage*, a *Business Week* best seller that was published in eleven languages.

She received a BA in economics and English from Tufts University and an MBA from Harvard Business School.